San Diego
LOWRIDERS

San Diego
LOWRIDERS

A HISTORY OF
Cars and Cruising

ALBERTO LÓPEZ PULIDO & RIGOBERTO "RIGO" REYES

THE
History
PRESS

Published by The History Press
Charleston, SC
www.historypress.net

First published 2017

ISBN 9781467137805

Library of Congress Control Number: 2016961488

CONTENTS

Acknowledgements

We wish to thank the San Diego Lowrider Council, which supported this book from its inception. We express our gratitude to the numerous individuals who came forward from the outset and supported this project with their images and stories, including Rudy Cervantes from Nosotros Car Club and Rachael Ortiz from the Barrio Station. In addition, we would like to thank Nicholas Aguilera from Diego & Son Printing. Mathias Ponce, aka "the Eagle," was so generous in sharing some of the earliest expressions of Chicano car culture. His images and story gave us a new understanding of the history of lowriding in San Diego. In addition, so many people were generous with their time and knowledge: Louie Ayala, Gilbert Reyes, Roumaldo "Mando" Romero, Chayo Colmenero, Gilbert Ochoa, Javier Rodriguez, Luis "Louie" Camacho, Sammy Mendoza, Pablo Chavez, Miguel Maestre, Carlos Contreras, Jesús "Chato" Esperza, Guillermo "Willie" Estrada, Rolando Mazon, Carlos Vasquez, Leo Hernandez, Richie Burgos, Mary Kamatoy, David Aguilar, Arturo Casares, Leo Hernandez, Phillip "Peabody" Gomez, Henry Rodriguez, Alex "Cabby" Flores, Jesús "Chacho" Amezcua, Ernie Carrillo, Ray Ramirez, Dave Diaz, Augie Bareno, Edwardo Corona, Miguel Croce, Toby Martinez, Lisandro Ponce, George Rodriguez, Carlos LeGerrette, Jose Arteaga, Hector Eribez, Arturo "Zorro" Herrera, Armando Medina, Robert Bryan, Ray Ulloa, Larry Flores, Manuel "Meño" Careño, Victor Cordero, Elsa Castillo, Jo Anna Samora-Harris, Nonie Samano, Diana Gonzalez, Allen "Butch" Sherman, Ben Osorio, George Yosif, Raymond Juarez, Steve "Masa" Wade, Raul Rodriguez and Joaquin Flores, Carol Raymond and Mary T. Kamatoy.

It is critically important that we acknowledge all the lowrider car clubs from the era, although for a variety of reasons outside of our control, some were not included in this book: the Stylistics, Life, Shades of the '50s, Latin Pride Car Club North County, Members Car Club of North County, Visions North County, the Elegants, Midnight Cruisers, Latin Image, South Side Lowriders, Royal Breed, Ebony, Internationals, De'Ville's Car Club, San Diego Car Club, Night Riders North County, Style Car Club and Escondido Car Club, among several others. We affirm their existence and thank them for their numerous contributions to San Diego lowriding.

This project would have never been completed without the skillful and gracious support from Keily Becerra, who was integral in helping us put this book together. Annie Ross, with an editorial eye and unwavering support in the belief of preserving community through history, made this book project possible. Allen Wynar, digital graphic arts professional in the Department of Instructional Technical Services at the University of San Diego, offered much of his time and guidance with some of the images in the book. We are grateful for the assistance of Marvin Israel Berechyahu Mayorga and for his photographs that he allowed us to include in this publication. The staff at Copley Library on the campus of the University of San Diego assisted us. Dean Theresa Byrd, university archivist Diane Maher, Special Collections manager Rachel Lieu and library assistant Rick Stoppelmoor were so helpful. We also wish to thank Lynda Claassen and Cristela Garcia-Spitz from UC San Diego's Digital Library Program. Administrators and staff from the University of San Diego, in particular Noelle Norton, Andrew Allen, Chris Nayve, James Harris, Debbie Gough and Esther Aguilar, were extremely helpful. The staff and board of directors of Via International have been instrumental in supporting this project from the outset. Under the leadership and guidance of Elisa Sabatini, Via International provided a space for us to share and discuss the importance of lowriding in the community. We are also indebted to filmmaker and friend Kelly Whalen, who guided so much of our initial film project and helped us bring together critical ideas and questions that have served to organize this book. Maria E. García, Tommie Camarillo, Josephine Talamantez, Jesse Constancio, Ramon "Chunky" Sanchez and Ruby Beltran were generous with their stories and guidance. We also thank and appreciate the dedicated service of the Chicano Park Steering Committee. We are grateful for the support from Ivy Westmoreland, who assisted in reading and writing a couple of the car club's histories. This project was initiated with encouragement from Megan Laddusaw and carefully guided and supported by Krista Slavicek, both acquisition editors with The History Press. In addition, Julia Turner's impressive editorial skills and Artie Crisp's support must also be acknowledged. A big thank-you goes to both, along with the rest of the staff at the press.

Alberto wishes to thank his wife, Yolanda Ramsey, and the Pulido, Valdez and Ramsey families for their love and support; his compadres Jose Hernandez and Antonio "Tony" Torres; his ethnic studies students and colleagues at the University of San Diego; and his partner in crime, Rigoberto Reyes, who was instrumental in bringing together so many from the San Diego lowrider world.

Rigoberto would like to thank his mother, Eustolia Reyes Jimenez, for her support throughout the years and his lowrider family for this opportunity to share the many stories of the car clubs in the San Diego, California region. He would like to acknowledge fallen brothers who had a great effect and influence on him and others: Chris Rodriguez from Brown Image, Arturo "Chuco" Ruiz from Latin Lowriders, Juan Rangel from Brown Image, Gaspar "Grandpa" Martinez from Amigos, Raul "El Indio" Guerrero from Amigos, Jose "Munchies" Ramirez from Klique, Juan Cuervo from Individuals, Maynard McBroom from Amigos and many others who are no longer with us. Thanks to them, we continue to promote this unique automotive culture we call lowriders. He would also like to express his deepest gratitude to Dr. Alberto López Pulido for his interest and determination in exposing the richness and extensive history of this underrepresented community to the world.

The purpose of this book is to document the early roots and history of San Diego lowriding. As a result, we do not address in detail lowrider movements and expression at the present moment. Yet we wish to salute those lowrider car clubs that appeared on the lowrider scene after 1985, such as Majestics Car Club, and all other lowrider car clubs that continue to make their marks in San Diego lowrider history and will be the future of lowriding in the twenty-first century and beyond.

Overview and Characteristics of the Lowrider Movement

Our cars have the color. Our cars have the character.
Our cars have what people talk about.
—*Ernie Carrillo, Classics Car Club*

The advent of automobile customization blossomed after the Second World War in the United States. It was driven by a desire to change and transform stock automobiles that were coming off the assembly line and make them distinctively one's own through creative customization. High-performance vehicles with radically altered bodies, custom paint jobs and unique interiors were quite the craze for car enthusiasts in countless cities throughout the United States during the 1950s. However, for working-class Chicano communities throughout the American Southwest, a distinct version of this car customization movement caught fire and began to take shape. In contrast to racing cars with big tires that conveyed a message of "fast and mean," the Chicano community began to imagine and create elegant and stylized vehicles with clean lines and small tires that were low to the ground. These cars came to be known as lowriders. Lowrider automobiles were imagined and customized to convey sentiments of "low and slow," which exemplified the cultural identity of their owners. While it is true that lowered vehicles were part of the overall custom car movement, Chicano lowriders radically transformed the roots of car customization because they came out of the unique culture and style of Mexican and Chicano barrios. For us to understand Chicano lowriding, we must first understand Chicano culture.

Cars from various car clubs lined up for a car show on Chicano Park Day in 1979. *Courtesy of Chacho Amezcua.*

Mathias Ponce's 1939 Chevy two door. This car is notable for its customized skirts over the back tires. *Courtesy of Mathias Ponce.*

Chicano lowriding begins with feelings of pride, *orgullo*, and respect, *respeto*, for self, community and culture. Respect for oneself is linked to self-love and personal worth, *amor propio*. An individual who possesses these values and sentiments is said to be *una persona educada*, or "an educated person," in a holistic sense. Pride, respect and self-love are at the root of lowrider expressions in the Chicano community, and realizing this helps us better understand this remarkable cultural movement. This combination of feelings reveals why people come together, create car clubs and spend countless hours adorning and transforming their cars to make them uniquely their own—ultimately becoming part of a larger collective movement.

THE EIGHT QUALITIES OF LOWRIDING

Pride, respect and self-love are distinctive Chicano values that are reflected in the lowriders' relationships with their vehicles. Through numerous years of being associated with the lowrider movement as members, organizers and/or filmmakers, we have come to discover eight unique qualities of lowriding.

1) *A creative spirit.* With limited resources and money, lowriders rely on creativity to achieve their desired artistic and mechanical vision. This artistic and mechanical inventiveness is defined as Chicano or Mexican ingenuity. The early introduction, adaptation and evolution of hydraulics in the lowrider community is an excellent example of this.
2) *An independent spirit.* The lowrider vehicle is a site of no boundaries. First, the impressive paint jobs and overall artistry put into the vehicle make a strong statement about freedom of expression. Secondly, driving the vehicle, "taking to the streets," is a physical representation of dismissing boundaries and restrictions. A lowrider vehicle becomes a moving piece of art as it takes to the streets and highways, making a statement by its unique composition. The lowrider experience is also a movement and a journey with the distinctive expression of low and slow as it transforms and challenges both space and time.
3) *Cultural pride with historic moments of cultural renaissance.* The adornment and modification of the lowrider vehicle manifest the specific culture of the Chicano and Mexicano lifestyle of pride and respect. Specific moments in history are connected to these expressions. For example, artwork of

Chicano cultural items and historical events increased on lowriders during the era of the Chicano civil rights struggle, known as the Chicano movement. In addition, these historical moments define the dress, fashion and styles of music embraced by this community.

4) *Activism in keeping Chicano lowrider culture alive and vibrant.* The lowrider community responds to the challenges coming from the dominant culture by promoting its culture even more emphatically. This explains the intense pride exhibited by car club members and the renaissance the movement is experiencing today.

5) *Community service.* The lowrider car clubs have a strong shared value of helping others. It is the motivating factor that brings people together to provide services for others. Community outreach can be anything from toy drives to fundraising efforts for illness or untimely deaths of friends and family. Lowriders are a very tightknit community in which people will gather in a matter of hours to provide support or to address a need or a crisis.

6) *Collectivism.* Lowriding is very personal, but it also honors the larger community. Community focus is at the core of why people come together and participate in picnics, dances and anniversaries. The lowrider community is a family; members are part of a brother- or sisterhood.

7) *Mindful of traditions and rituals.* This speaks to the evolution of lowrider expression and representation. As lowriding continues to evolve and develop throughout various communities and throughout the world, there are new and different forms of expressions emerging that are changing the lowrider movement as we know it at present. This book concludes with a brief reflection on the changing face of lowrider after 1985 along with a reflection on the internationalization of the lowrider movement.

8) *Cultural continuity.* As the pioneers of lowriding become older and less active, there is a strong desire and need to impart lowrider culture and expressions to the next generation. This transgenerational sentiment represents one of the central reasons for writing this book. We hope the future of lowriding can be built and developed on the stories, expressions and hard work that was established by the pioneers of lowriding in San Diego and the borderlands.

To summarize, the values of creativity, independence, pride, activism, community service, collectivism, attention to traditions and cultural continuity are presented in the stories told throughout this book.

OVERVIEW OF BOOK

Lowrider magazine was established in the mid-1970s and is the most well-known lowrider publication, selling more newsstand copies than any other car magazine in the United States. The magazine has gone through numerous changes and is currently being published by the Enthusiast Network in Anaheim, California. In October 2015, the magazine broke new ground by introducing editorial changes. It announced the removal of all bikini-clad female models from its pages, and instead, there would be a focus on the "art of lowrider car building and Hispanic automotive culture." The magazine identified what it calls the four pillars of lowriding for understanding lowrider culture: 1) performance, 2) artistry, 3) pride and 4) culture. While such changes are to be commended for keeping the lowrider movement alive, it is important to note the overarching pillar that acknowledges the power of story and history of lowriding is missing. It is impossible to speak about the performance, artistry, pride and culture of the lowrider community without embedding these pillars within a history of the community. Hence, telling the story of lowriding is the main reason for writing this book. Our objective is to honor the

Mathias Ponce poses next to his lowered vehicle, a 1939 Chevy two door. *Courtesy of Mathias Ponce.*

history of lowriding in San Diego by documenting the stories of all who participated.

San Diego Lowriders: A History of Cars and Cruising captures Chicano lowrider history between the years 1950 and 1985. It unearths and captures the histories of twenty-eight lowrider car clubs that are responsible for the establishment of lowriding in this Southern California city along the U.S.-Mexico border. We refer to this region as the borderlands. We feature the stories of lowrider car clubs that have never been documented. This includes exclusively female car clubs and lowrider car clubs from Tijuana, Mexico. Through a chronological history of the movement, we document the earliest evidence of lowriders, which begin in 1950. We conclude in 1985, when the act of cruising became outlawed and lowriding began to change from its original form and style. Our goal is to capture the unique and evolving trends of lowriding over time.

Our book begins with the distinctive characteristics and features of San Diego lowriding that we describe as the *raíces*, or "roots," of the movement. We continue with a discussion of the foundational organized lowrider car clubs that arrived on the San Diego street scene in the late 1960s and early 1970s. This is followed by a period that is marked by the emergence of a unique lowrider identity in this borderlands region on both sides of the U.S.-Mexico border. This period, between 1972 and 1974, is marked by the first signs of contact and sponsorship between lowrider car clubs in both San Diego and Tijuana, Mexico. The chronology continues by documenting the evolving and changing dynamic of the lowrider movement, including organized car-hops, and then moves into a discussion of the changing lowrider cultural aesthetics between old and new vehicles. We follow with a discussion of female lowriders, who have arrived on scene by the early 1980s. In addition, the years 1980–85 mark the end of an era for the foundational lowrider movement with the systematic shutting down of cruising street zones by law enforcement, a significant moment in lowrider history, as the movement is taken off the streets and into the car show venue. We conclude with a reflection on the future of lowriding in a global society where it has moved beyond its traditional space of the Chicano barrios and into the hearts and minds of car communities throughout the world.

LOWRIDING AS LOCAL HISTORY

San Diego Lowriders: A History of Cars and Cruising is organized around the belief that the most important history to be written is local. It highlights the fact that history occurs in a physical place. Be it parks, clubhouses, parking lots, the streets of San Diego or the car shows or beaches of Tijuana, Mexico, the story of the lowrider movement happened in a place that is both local and real. By focusing on "lowrider places," we highlight the local history and cultural expressions that come out of such places. Therefore, in telling the history of lowriding, which emerged from the Chicano barrios in San Diego, California, we identify three levels of space that organize and guide lowrider life and living: 1) gathering places, 2) vehicles and 3) activities performed within spaces. We believe this best captures the life of living "low-n-slow" in the heart of the borderlands and affirms the eight qualities of lowriding outlined previously. In addition, each chapter includes a brief insert called "Street Vistas" in which a key feature of lowrider experiences and expressions is highlighted.

San Diego Lowriders: A History of Cars and Cruising tells the story of this fascinating and rich movement that at best is unknown and at worst is misunderstood and stereotyped. Our story moves us beyond "gang-banging" depictions that evoke fear in the hearts of many and instead presents a counter-history that honors and recognizes the unique qualities and contributions of this movement of cars that has profoundly influenced the automotive world across the globe. We invite you to cruise with us through the San Diego lowrider movement's history and learn its rich and vibrant story.

1

LAS RAÍCES

The Early Roots of Lowriding in San Diego, 1950-68

MATHIAS PONCE AND THE ART OF LOWRIDING

Serra Car Club of Old Town and Bean Bandits of San Diego

The early *raíces* of lowriding in San Diego, California, began in the 1950s, with people having a desire to come together to acquire vehicles and share ideas on how best to modify vehicles in creative and unique ways. A sizeable portion of these activities were motivated by "hanging out," working on cars, cruising and racing cars and simply socializing with a desire to build community and to establish close and long-lasting friendships. These activities were at the core of the early car cultures that have persisted into the present period. We begin our journey with one of the most influential individuals in the lowrider movement. Mathias Ponce came onto the car scene in the 1940s in the community of Old Town in San Diego, California. He was a car enthusiast, speed and drag racer and, most significant for our project, a lowrider. As a young man, Mathias began lowering and cruising cars as early as the late 1940s throughout San Diego. He was a proud member of the Serra Car Club, considered to be the very first car club that welcomed and supported lowriders and lowriding in San Diego and anywhere else for that matter. Based in Old Town, the car club held its meetings at the Old Town Recreational Center in the shadows of Presidio Park. The club chose its name from the Catholic missionary Father Junipero Serra and had up to fifteen members. One of the favorite activities

Above: Mathias Ponce poses on top of his customized 1939 Chevy four door in Bay Park. The vehicle has hubcaps that came from a 1956 Chrysler. *Courtesy of Mathias Ponce.*

Left: A woman poses in front of the Old Town Recreation Hall, where the Serra Car Club gathers. *Courtesy of Mathias Ponce.*

of the Serra Car Club was cruising the streets of Linda Vista and Mission Beach with limited contact with the communities of southern San Diego.

A good part of Mathias's car and cruising activities included his younger brother David. They would imagine new ways to customize their cars and share them when they hung out with friends and other club members. The Ponce brothers—Mathias, David and Ernie—were well known in the San Diego region for their cars and their friendship. In the community, they were known as "good guys."

One of their most popular hangouts was at Presidio Park, where they proudly displayed their vehicles on the lawn in front of the Presidio in the 1950s.

Mathias's lowriding journey began when he was a young man in the early 1940s and was obligated to help his brother with collecting and selling "junk"—what he refers to as "junking." It was during one of these episodes of going through piles of unwanted materials that he discovered a square metal box. As he thought about this little box, he came up with an idea: to place it between the back springs and rear end of his car. (This will lower the rear end of the car.) Mathias was self-taught on the mechanics of suspension systems on cars because he had to fix his brother's car, whose

David Ponce's 1953 Coupe de Ville facing Mathias Ponce's 1950 Mercury at Presidio Park in San Diego. *Courtesy of Mathias Ponce.*

rear end had broken, and discovered how rear ends of cars worked. Later, he would discover aluminum blocks that could be used to create the same effect. This Mexican ingenuity served him well; the lowering block concept was taught to many young lowriders and became a common practice until well into the 1970s. Another lowering method that was not always preferred was heating up the back springs that bolted to the back of the car. The heat compresses the springs, lowering the car.

The desire to lower his vehicles was based on performance—they simply rode better that way. American cars built during the 1940s and '50s were very large, and the car rode very high off the ground. Mathias noticed that lots of air would get underneath the cars and they would not handle very well. So he figured that by lowering the car, you could eliminate the air, allowing for a much smoother and more gentle ride. Mathias became very well known in the region for lowering cars, and before you knew it, he was in high demand throughout Southern California, where numerous car enthusiasts would hire him to lower their cars.

Mathias Ponce poses with his Bean Bandits Racing Team jacket. *Courtesy of Alberto Pulido.*

By 1965, Mathias had begun to drag race and became known as *el Águila*, or "the Eagle," in the drag racing world. He would own a total of three different dragsters—created and customized by him—throughout his career. Mathias's involvement in the drag racing scene led him to get involved with the Bean Bandits, a resourceful and amazing racing team founded in 1949. Joaquin Arnett Jr., described by many as a mechanical genius, guided this predominantly Mexican American racing team to win nearly four hundred trophies at the height of its presence in the racing world. In addition to Ponce and Arnett, other members, such as Robert Martinez, were recognized for their brilliance and skill in customizing vehicles.

Throughout all their visionary work, the Bean Bandits' modification and lowering of cars drew much attention and gave them much notoriety that would influence the next generation of lowrider customizers. Their unique vehicles and bright yellow jackets were popular and respected in the Mexican barrio of Logan Heights in San Diego.

Street Vistas
Lowriding Culture and Music

An integral part of the lowrider movement is cultural pride. We identify it as one of the eight qualities of lowriding in the introduction. In addition to lifestyle and dress, music is central to the lowrider experience. Numerous styles, including rhythm and blues, soul, traditional Mexican music and "oldies but goodies," have been central to lowrider culture and community. A common activity of all the lowrider car clubs featured here are dances. Dances were always being organized by numerous car clubs, and some car clubs became extremely popular for the dances they organized and bands they featured. Clubs usually designed their own tickets and posters to publicize the event, and these became part of the

A poster for a dance sponsored and organized by Brown Image Car Club. *Courtesy of Rachael Ortiz.*

David Ponce and Rosie Hamlin of Rosie and the Originals at a car show in Balboa Park featuring Mathias Ponce's motorcycle, the "Untouchable." *Courtesy of Mathias Ponce.*

art of the lowrider movement. The practice of organizing dances for the community began in the 1950s with social clubs during the early roots of lowriding. A good example of a social club is represented by Los Lobos, which is discussed in this chapter.

The "oldies but goodies" scene cannot be more clearly accented than by the song "Angel Baby" by Rosie and the Originals. Rosie Hamlin spent part of her youth in National City, where she wrote the lyrics to the song that featured Mathias Ponce's brother David as one of the guitarists of the group.

THE ORIGINAL LOS LOBOS JACKET CLUB OF LOGAN HEIGHTS

Social clubs, known as jacket clubs, were an important part of youth culture during the 1950s in the community of Logan Heights and surrounding communities in San Diego. They instilled great pride and

YOU ARE CORDIALLY INVITED TO ATTEND THE

LOS LOBOS

2nd. ANNUAL

HOLIDAY DANCE

FEATURING

Gayniters 3 Solid Senders

WAR MEMORIAL BUILDING

NOVEMBER 29, 1957   DONATION .90

8 TO 12   CASUAL DRESS

A dance ticket sponsored by Los Lobos Jacket Club. *Courtesy of Gilbert Reyes.*

provided leadership skills for Mexican American men from this era. Several of the jackets clubs came out of the local neighborhood house. The neighborhood house had been in existence since the 1920s and provided key social services, cultural activities and community-building opportunities for Logan Heights. Among the many clubs that emerged during this era were Los Gallos, Los Chicanos and Los Lobos. The majority of these clubs had some incredible mentorship from community leaders such as Al Pelón Johnson, and Coaches Merlin Pinkerton and Frank Galindo worked incessantly with the youth of Logan Heights. One of the most important contributions of the jacket clubs was their social function in the community. They were organized to build community and practice the value of reciprocity. Here we find the roots of lowrider qualities and expressions as outlined in the introduction. It is important to note that key, active women's social clubs, such as the Blue Velvets and the Shebas, also represent a part of this history, but unfortunately, they have not received the same amount of notoriety as their all-male counterparts. Like with other jackets clubs from this era, a major activity organized by Los Lobos were dances. As noted in this chapter, music was an integral part of the Chicano and Mexican American experience through organized dances with live bands. They were fun times for people to gather, socialize, date and dance to the rhythm of the live music.

In 1954, (*left to right*) Joe Ortega, David Ayala and Raymond Herrera of Los Lobos Jacket Club pose in front of a 1937–38 Chevy. *Courtesy of Gilbert Reyes.*

Lobos Jacket Club members (*left to right*) Roumaldo "Mando" Romero, Gilbert Reyes and Chayo Colmenero pose with the original Los Lobos fingertip jacket. *Courtesy of Alberto Pulido.*

The jacket clubs are critical for lowrider history because they were how the emerging lowrider scene and aesthetic began to proliferate. The style and type of vehicles that were designed during this era were similar to those customized by car enthusiasts such as Mathias Ponce. In fact, some of Los Lobos friends and members who owned vehicles remember they acquired their first car from Mathias. As Louie Ayala recalled, "Mathias was the guy with the '39 Chevy coupes." Dress and fashion, in particular the jackets adorned by members of these social clubs, became the pattern adopted and worn by the lowrider car clubs up to the present day. The type and style of jacket, along with the lettering on both the front and back of the jacket, have become a signature lowrider trait. With the importance of style and representation, looking sharp and taking great pride in one's appearance was of great importance to Los Lobos. As Gilbert Reyes, a cofounder of Los Lobos Jacket Club, looked around and saw that all the other clubs had what are known as stadium jackets, with the ribbed collar and waist, he sought to do something very different. The jacket he designed was long and stylish and gave the club members a unique quality. Friends and family were very impressed with the jackets. The founding members of Los Lobos were Gilbert Reyes, Phillip Usquiano, Rudy Gomez, Louie Boreno, David Fuentes and Robert Delgado, who began the club in 1953 as students at Memorial Junior High in someone's garage. By 1954, Los Lobos had moved to the neighborhood house, where they remained throughout their history.

Los Villanos of San Ysidro

Guided and inspired by his father, Gilbert Ochoa learned a great deal about car customizing in his father's garage, supplied with plenty of tools and cutting torches. He became very popular with his friends in the small community of San Ysidro on the U.S.-Mexico border, about fourteen miles south of Logan Heights in the area popularly known as south San Diego or the South Bay. By sharing tools and becoming skilled with his father's cutting torch, Ochoa and several of his friends began to gather and hang out in his father's garage in the late 1950s. By 1958, they had become known as Los Villanos of San Ysidro, California. Members included Harvey Acosta, Armando Garcia, Art Palacios, Frank Parra, Rafael Armas, Robert Montoya, Phil Reyes and Gilbert Ochoa. They represented one of the first documented custom car

In 1957, Gilbert Ochoa of Los Villanos Car Club on his 1948 Plymouth two-door sedan in San Ysidro, California. *Courtesy of Gilbert Ochoa.*

clubs in the South Bay region. The lowering method used by this Mexican car club was one resembling a "California Rake" style, lowering more in the front than in the rear of the vehicle, which was very popular during this era. In Spanish, they referred to these cars as *pinacates*, referring to the popular

Gilbert Ochoa poses with Los Villanos Car Club plaque. *Courtesy of Alberto Pulido.*

stink bug beetle with large populations in the borderlands region. These car customizers were all about modifying their vehicles for the sake of racing performance with an eye toward having the fastest car in the region. Like with other car clubs, Los Villanos also sponsored dances in order to raise funds and bring the community together. Their favorite hangout was George's Drive-In on the corner of Palm and Thirteen Avenues in the neighboring community of Imperial Beach. Members of Los Villanos found themselves in Imperial Beach at least five days a week because San Ysidro did not have a high school, so they had to attend Mar Vista High School in Imperial Beach. Gilbert loved to drive their cars or motorcycles to high school and loved to hang out at George's, socializing and displaying their vehicles for all to see. By 1960, the club had disbanded, but it reconstituted soon after with Anglo members from Imperial Beach. They remained together until 1962.

COACHMEN OF SAN YSIDRO

Another group of car customizers to come out of San Ysidro were the Coachmen Car Club. Led by Sammy Mendoza and Pablo Chávez, the Coachmen Car Club began to gather in 1964 as classmates from Southwest Junior High. There were ten original members. They describe their early days as a bunch of guys getting together to build and fix up cars. They would gather as a group to collectively troubleshoot mechanical problems and to exchange ideas on how to build more efficient and faster cars. The Coachmen did not own lowriders. They took their name and logo from the Fisher brothers, who were coach builders at the turn of the twentieth century in Detroit, Michigan, and had a division of General Motors named for them. They did not become an official car club organization until 1965,

The original Coachmen Car Club members: Sammy Mendoza, Pablo Chavez and Miguel Maestre. *Courtesy of Keily Becerra.*

when a young community organizer by the name of Delia Camacho stepped in to help them legally incorporate in response to law enforcement agents who constantly ticketed them for "disorderly gatherings" when they hung out at the popular civic center and park in the heart of San Ysidro. The club was attracted to the park because of its large trees, which provided shade for them as they cleaned and waxed their cars. Their incorporation as an official car club curtailed police oversight and gave them legitimacy. Their customizing efforts were put into building hot rods for speed and high performance. They were good friends with many of the mechanic shops in the region, such as Crower Cams, and were willing to test out new parts to see how well they performed in their vehicles. These Mexican teenagers from the small town of San Ysidro were very united and shared knowledge, money and talent to build some great modified vehicles. They were mentored and guided by Charlie Salcedo, who was the president of the Tijuana Drag Racing Association, and they spent a lot of time racing their modified vehicles in the border town of Tecate, Mexico. The original Coachmen Car Club disbanded around 1969 as the young men grew older and married. The car club reconstituted itself from 1972 to 1974, and then a third Coachmen Car Club came onto the scene in 2005 and remains active today.

The Original Baja Kings of Logan Heights

Along with his two friends Mike Paz and Patrociño Calderon, Javier Ramirez got the idea of starting a car club in the late 1960s. All three were classmates at Memorial Junior High in Logan Heights. According to Javier, their main reason for coming together as a car club was for them to feel good about themselves. Initially, people did not take them seriously—many felt it was some sort of a joke. Having anticipated such a reception to his plan, Javier had a solution. He would invite the most popular kid to join the club—Luis "Louie" Camacho. It also helped that Louie was Javier's best friend. Javier's plan worked. Louie gave the club legitimacy, and within three weeks, the Baja Kings had fifty members. The original plan of the club was to accept only members who owned Chevrolets. But with time, anyone would be allowed into the club as long as they could pay their dues in the amount of one dollar per meeting. The Baja Kings was unlike any other car club described in this book. First, none of the members owned a lowrider. Their limited degree of car customizing was related directly to the limited resources from the membership. All the members

A poster for a dance organized and hosted by the Baja Kings of Logan Heights. *Courtesy of Rachael Ortiz.*

attended school full time and worked minimum-wage jobs. But showing one of the eight unique qualities of lowriding, the membership possessed a great deal of Mexican ingenuity and did a lot with limited resources. One of the characteristics of lowriding popular with the Baja Kings was the creation and installation of the plaque in the rear window of the vehicle that became a common trait in the lowrider world. Although their cars were not the most customized of vehicles, the car plaque drew much attention to the club and was popular in attracting members of the opposite sex, according to Javier.

One of the most notable qualities of the Baja Kings Car Club was that the majority of the membership was from Mexico. As described by Javier, they were the "new arrivals" who spoke strictly Spanish. As they interacted with the Chicano population from Logan, they quickly discovered that they were made to feel different and stand out. In their

Street Vistas
The Lowrider Car Club Plaque

A distinguishing characteristic of lowrider car culture is the unique car plaque. The early car clubs created these plaques by designing them and casting them in brass. In so many ways, the decision of a club to move forward with the creation of a plaque marked its beginning. Much of the early work of individuals creating a car club includes the planning and creation of a car plaque and the name of the new club. The plaque represents the heart of the car club and reflects what the club stands for; it is a determining factor whether a club will survive. A plaque is taken very seriously, and much respect goes into the display of the plaque and how members revere it. Only club members have the right to fly and show the plaque, and they should not fly a plaque if their car is dirty, crashed or damaged in any way. The plaque is all about representation. It embodies a sense of belonging, pride and personal affirmation.

The Casinos Car Club plaque of south San Diego. *Courtesy of Rigo Reyes.*

words, the *pochos* did not always care for them to the point that the Mexican kids would gather in a designated place before school and walk together for protection. Furthermore, differences were reinforced by the neighborhood schools, which offered very little instruction in Spanish. By the time the kids entered Memorial Junior High School, they were forced to band together to have a sense self-worth and respect. In many ways, the organizing by these young men, as well as that of their female friends, was to claim turf. To claim their own space within Logan Heights among the Chicanos and outside of Logan with other ethnic groups from neighboring communities. According to Javier, the Baja Kings became so popular that they swelled to 150 members and friends who loved to hang out with them. In his mind, at the height of the club's popularity Baja Kings was synonymous with Logan Heights. Like the majority of the car clubs, the Baja Kings sponsored dances in the community and was probably the first club to socialize and gather with another club, known as Los Duendes, from Tijuana, Mexico. Los Duendes was known for its popular *bailes al revés*, or "reverse dances," where the women took the men out to dance. There was no official sponsorship between San Diego and Tijuana clubs, but nonetheless, there was a lot of interaction—not always the best— between the two car clubs. They would establish the model for future San Diego lowrider car clubs. The club had disbanded by the early '70s as the members became older with new opportunities and changes in their lives.

This *raíces* era of lowrider history introduces the early qualities of lowriding that remain with us until this day. During this period, there is a mixture of lowrider cars and hot rods as members of these San Diego *barrios* would come to discover their distinctive contributions to the overall car customization movement and through the process come to know themselves. The emergence and representation of these clubs was all about affirming their place in San Diego and the broader U.S. societies. This underscores many of the qualities outlined in the introduction regarding lowrider culture. We now move on to the next stage in San Diego lowrider history, which features the lowrider *clicas*, or car clubs, and their unique expressions and aesthetics.

2

CLICAS

Foundational Lowrider Car Clubs, 1969-71

C *lica* is commonly used among the lowrider community to mean a car club or clique. It utilizes a particular form of language from the borderlands region referred to as Caló, in which Spanish and English are combined to create a new, distinct language. It is commonly utilized by lowrider car clubs and the broader Chicano community. In a broader meaning, *clica* refers to the sense of belonging to something larger than oneself—the brotherhood/sisterhood as outlined in the eight qualities of lowriding. It is all about the reinforcement and expression of the culture. *Clica* is introduced here as a way to mark the creative spirit and ingenuity by lowrider car clubs from this time that established the foundational era of lowriding.

NOSOTROS CAR CLUB OF LOGAN HEIGHTS

The first car club formed in the foundational lowrider era in San Diego came via Barrio Station, a community agency in Logan Heights. Barrio Station was established in 1969–70 with an eye toward meeting the needs of the community and offered free after-school activities with the intent of discouraging "delinquency, youth violence and gang involvement and in turn encourage civic responsibility and successful school performance." Under the direction of Rachael Ortiz, Barrio Station remains an active youth center with the idea that it can make the neighborhood safer and

Nosotros Car Club members pose with their car club jacket. *Courtesy of Rudy Cervantes.*

enhance children's sense of community pride and a realization of their own positive capabilities through structured activities. It is out of this context that the first organized and foundational car club in San Diego emerged.

Nosotros Car Club was established in the early 1970s. At the height of the club, Nosotros attracted fifteen members, including Rudy Cervantes, Ben Pasana, Rudy Rodriguez, Alex Martinez, Joseph Ortega, Gonzalo Carrillo and Willie Rios. The car club was established with the intent of attracting members by assisting them in devoting time and resources to repair and display their automobiles for personal and public admiration. It sought to reinforce that long-standing Mexican and Chicano value of supporting and helping community youth. The Nosotros Car Club would gather weekly at Barrio Station. The club organized a car clinic in response to members from the community who lacked the resources for custom paint jobs and upholstery.

The car club was highly organized and conducted business in accordance to Roberts Rules of Order. It collected dues and had officers, such as a president, vice-president, treasurer and secretary. The club had nominations and elections for officers, along with campaign speeches in which candidates articulated the vision of the club. The principal goal

Rudy Cervantes of Nosotros
Car Club. *Courtesy of Rudy
Cervantes.*

of the club was to produce one car that was nice enough to display at a major San Diego car show. As the club evolved, this goal began to change as the members felt that they had not produced many standout vehicles and, more importantly, had not produced a lowrider. As one of the founding members of Nosotros Car Club, Rudy Cervantes, noted, the most important "vehicle" to come out of Nosotros Car Club was actually more visionary, as the club stressed the importance of involving themselves in the broader, sometimes political, activities of the community. Rather than builders of special cars, Nosotros members were first and foremost identified as "community helpers," playing the role of peacekeepers with an emphasis on bringing the community together. Through Barrio Station, Nosotros Car Club members became mentors and big brothers to a youth group known as Los Hermanos. Members of the brotherhood organized and chaperoned fundraising dances and car washes for the group.

The objective of Nosotros Car Club was to create activities that would focus on helping the community and how, collectively, the community could help the youth engage in positive activities. As a result, Nosotros members were always very careful of the reputation they put forward, recognizing that they were not only representing Nosotros car club but also Barrio Station and the overall Chicano community of Logan Heights. The support from

The members of Nosotros Car Club were well known for their engagement with the youth of the barrio. They were especially known for their bike activities, as exemplified in this photograph. *Courtesy of Rudy Cervantes.*

Barrio Station was very important because it provided a space for meetings, organizational support and connection to local resources. At one point, Barrio Station moved into a new and larger facility that had an adjoining garage that Nosotros was able to use for numerous community activities. Nosotros ran a community car clinic where local residents could work on their cars. The clinic offered professional mechanic tools and an air compressor that was acquired through local small grants.

One of the most successful club programs was a no-cost bicycle repair clinic for preteens and teens. It was supported by Barrio Station, the 4-H Organization and the San Diego Police Department. With bicycle parts donated by the police department, club members provided mechanical assistance to upgrade the bikes and keep them in safe working condition. This program was highly successful and culminated each year with a community bike show at which youth exhibited their customized and tricked bicycles.

As the members became older and the community began to change, many members left the club and went on to establish their own influential lowrider car clubs.

Latin Lowriders Car Club of Southeast San Diego

The Latin Lowrider Car Club began at the end of the 1960s. The founding members were Ray Tirado, Jimmy Mendoza, John Hansen, Phillip "Peabody" Gomez, Freddy Alcaraz, Ralph Rosmob, Lisandro Ponce, Gabe Campa, Arturo "Chuco" Ruiz, Johnny Reyes, Albert Castañeda and Jaime Castañeda. Other key members who were only remembered by their first name were "Tochi" and "Baldy." The majority of these young men split from Nosotros Car Club and organized the first exclusively lowrider car club in San Diego. This marks an important moment in San Diego lowrider history because up to this point, all car clubs were a blend of lowrider vehicles and hot rods—a combination of racers and cruisers. Latin Lowriders would be the first organized car club to capture a distinctive style for lowriding

The Latin Lowriders Car Club taken in Playas de Tijuana. *Courtesy of Richie Burgos.*

This 1973 Montego belonged to Javier Fierro of Latin Lowriders Car Club. *Courtesy of Richie Burgos.*

that came to define this era. Historically, the Latin Lowriders embodied the civil rights values and actions that had swept up the youth from this period known as the Chicano movement. As a result, expressions of cultural pride and ethnic identity enfolded in a youthful lowrider car culture that became exclusively Chicano and barrio-based in San Diego. The club would hold its meetings at the newly established Chicano Park and at the Chicano Federation.

This characteristic lowrider style from the 1970s can be seen in some of their vehicles. Richard Acosta's 1964 Buick Riviera, painted a rich purple color, stands out as a classic '70s lowrider car. The Riviera (Rivi) vehicle was very popular among the lowrider community because it symbolized elegance and luxury. As Richie Burgos reflected, "It had everything you wanted in a vehicle." In addition to Acosta's striking paint job, this Rivi is lifted with hydraulics, the body is adorned with pinstripes and dual "LA show pipes." We also see the classic Cragar rims and the introduction of the smaller tire. With the tire situated deeply inside the well, the illusion that the car is lower (and therefore more stylish) is achieved. It was also popular to adorn these

This 1954 Chevy "Betzylu" was owned by Henry Lozano of Latin Lowriders Car Club. *Courtesy of Richie Burgos.*

wheel wells with interior lighting. Another very important vehicle from this era was Javier Fierro's 1973 Montego, known as "Montezuma's Revenge." In addition to its exceptional paint job and artistic expressions, Fierro's Montego has modifications similar to Acosta's "Rivi."

As with the majority of the other car clubs described in this book, the Latin Lowriders were very well known for their dances. They would hold several dances a year featuring the most popular musical groups from the era. They were also famous for their great barbecues that were popular with communities throughout San Diego. The club loved to cruise San Diego and Tijuana at the popular Playas de Tijuana—a beach community south of Tijuana commonly known as simply Playas. They would also attend dances in Tijuana and were sponsored by United Browns, a Mexican car club. This sponsorship, or *compadrazgo*, was vitally important in affirming these young men. During this era, there was very little support for the lowrider lifestyle in San Diego, and many faced scrutiny from law enforcement, which often questioned their value and right to exist on the streets of their hometown. The clubs and streets of Tijuana provided a refuge for many of the car clubs that literally crossed borders to validate their place in the automotive world.

It is also important to mention that the Latin Lowrider Car Club was the first to coordinate and organize the first lowrider car show on Chicano Park Day in 1978. These relationships and accompanying experiences proved to be invaluable in the lives of the club's members.

In 2014, the Latin Lowriders Car Club officially regrouped with ten to eleven members. All members are required to own a vehicle that meets the standards of lowriding within a more fluid club structure than in the past. All events are coordinated with the collective support and resources from club members. The most important aspect of the current club is that the members are genuinely interested in the vision and art of lowriding in its most traditional sense. Members range from thirty-five to sixty-five years of age with some being grandfathers and great-grandfathers. For the Latin Lowriders, the traditions continue!

CHICANO BROTHERS CAR CLUB OF NATIONAL CITY

Three young men—Leo Hernandez, Joe Sermeño and Mario Zaragoza—got together in the community of Paradise Hills in 1968 and were interested in starting some kind of car club. Since Citizen Band or CB radios were in fashion, they decided to call themselves the CBs. These young men hit the road with their CB radios and large antennas communicating among themselves and others. When friends and classmates learned about this new car club, the question arose, what does CB stand for? As Leo Hernandez reflected, "We were young and just coming out with our Chicano identity, so without much thought, we blurted, 'Chicano Brothers!'"

By late 1969, Chicano Brothers had come onto the lowrider car scene, and one of the most notable achievements of this car club was its success in locating and establishing a clubhouse. Along with Leo, Joe and Mario came a whole new set of guys from National City: Marcos Ruiz, Alfredo "Boo Boo" Martinez, Chuco Ruiz, Andres Gutierrez, "Redhead" Lorenzo, Ralph Nieblas, David Aguilar, Eddie Huerta, Rudy Martinez, Al Wilson and Bobby Loco. There was also a person by the name of Jay whose last name could not be recalled. The group had attracted quite a following, and the members were set on establishing a clubhouse. Through their search, they discovered an empty warehouse on the corner of Twenty-First and Roosevelt Streets in National City

From left to right: Ralph Nieblas, Leo Hernandez, Rudy Martinez and Andres Gutierrez of the Chicano Brothers Car Club. *Courtesy of Leo Hernandez.*

David Aguilar posing with his 1950 Chevy Fleetline in front of his parents' house in Otay, California. *Courtesy of David Aguilar.*

A poster for a dance organized and hosted by Chicano Brothers Car Club. *Courtesy of Rachael Ortiz.*

This 1964 White Impala belonged Leo Hernandez of Chicano Brothers Car Club. The picture was taken at their clubhouse in National City in 1970. *Courtesy of Leo Hernandez.*

Above: A recent picture of David Aguilar of Chicano Brothers in his car club jacket. *Courtesy of Keily Becerra.*

Left: David Aguilar shows off the back of his Chicano Brothers Car Club jacket. *Courtesy of Keily Becerra.*

and sought support to acquire it. They quickly contacted Luis "Louie" Camacho, who had recently been elected to the city council of National City. As a civic-minded politician who enjoyed supporting youth-oriented projects, Camacho quickly acted on obtaining this space for the Chicano Brothers, sponsoring the club and collecting a rental fee of one dollar a month. The newly established Chicano Brothers Club House was ideal: it had a full compressor, bathrooms and a recreation room with pool tables. Much of the customizing of the Chicano Brothers vehicles came out of their clubhouse through the ingenious mind of Bobby Loco. He is credited with painting many of the cars and assisting in creating the lowrider style from this era. On the weekend, the clubhouse became a very popular meeting place and hangout for clubs from throughout San Diego. There, they could gather and work on cars and share news of upcoming dances, cruises or happenings.

Through club member Ralph Nieblas, the Chicano Brothers spent a lot of time in Tijuana, Mexico, with the Tijuana car clubs El Grupo y Los Nosotros. Both clubs played a role in sponsoring the Chicano Brothers for numerous dances held in Tijuana at El Campestre, a popular nightspot. The favorite and most popular Tijuana hangout for the Chicano Brothers was Mike's, a historic nightclub and bar on Avenida Revolución. Just like all the other car clubs, the Chicano Brothers spent lots of time cruising Playas and hanging out with friends. The Chicano Brothers became very involved with community-minded work through their association with San Diego female social clubs. The Casualettes was an active social club in San Diego during this era and did a great deal of work sponsoring dances to support charities in Tijuana in addition to toy drives during the Christmas season. Eventually, members of the Chicano Brothers began to court members of the Casualettes, leading to marriage. The history of women's social clubs emerging from the barrio is an important one. Similar to the history of the women's clubs that emerged during the *raíces* era, more contemporary clubs such as the Chi-lites, Lady Elegants, Perlettes and Emeralds is a critical history that must be told. Their origins and association with lowrider car clubs added a new and necessary dimension to this history. The Chicano Brothers Car Club began to fade by 1973 as the members got older and life commitments such as marriage took over. Chicano Brothers Car Club often found themselves in turf wars with another National City–based club, Los Gatos from Old Town National City.

Brown Image Car Club of Logan Heights

Teddy Egipto and Chris Rodriguez were among the many male youths from the Logan Heights neighborhood who partook in both social and sports activities directly in the car club community. In the late 1960s, these young men wanted to formalize these friendships from the neighborhood during a time when all the excitement surrounding lowriding was alive and thriving. Teddy was the illustrator and master craftsman, and Chris was the administrator who possessed all the skills for launching a car club. What emerged was the Brown Image Car Club with a strong foundation and belief that this sense of "brotherhood" needed to be affirmed. As Henry Rodriguez proclaimed, "It was all about the lowrider; about the Mexican heritage." In addition to these strong bonds, there were strong feelings by people like Teddy, who would attend the popular "World of Wheels Car Show" organized by the car show promoter RG Canning. He noted that among the hundreds of cars on display, lowrider vehicles were visibly absent, which motivated him to organize a first-class lowrider car club. The first meeting of the Brown Image Car Club was held amid the tall cement pillars that would serve as canvases for the monumental murals of Chicano Park on

The founding members of the Brown Image Car Club. *Courtesy of Henry Rodriguez.*

Three members from the Brown Image Car Club with the original Brown Image plaque. *Courtesy of Henry Rodriguez.*

Dewey Street, which ran through the park in its early history. Along with Teddy and Chris, there were Delfino Perez, the brothers Paco and Pepe Alvarado, Juan Rangel, Chedo Flores, Phil Segarra, Carlos Juarez, Jessi Rios, Andy Alvaro, Negris and Lonley Romero, Joe and Nick Casillas, Alfonso Durazo, Jerry Estrada, Jaime Campuzano, Henry Camberos, Philip Clemente, Lalo Martinez, Ricky Cervantes and Mark Delaney, among many others. Brown Image was a highly organized lowrider car club. It developed elaborate club rules that guided the young car club members and showed extraordinary organizing skills, which afforded the club a great deal of respectability and popularity in the community. Out of this context came strong leadership with ideas and strategies on how to make the club stronger.

BROWN IMAGE CAR CLUB OFFICIAL RULES

RULES PERTAINING TO THE WEEKLY MEETINGS.

A) Meetings to begin promptly at 7:00 p.m. every Friday, unless otherwise changed by the President. (Fifty cent fine for tardiness.)

B) There will not be any smoking or drinking while a meeting is being held. (Fifty cent fine)

C) The Sergent-at-arms shall keep order and shall issue fines when members are out of order. Talking out of order is not tolerated, two warnings shall be issued to a member. After that he will be dismissed from the meeting.

D) Absences are not accepted, except if you have a valid reason, in which you should call one of the officers to be excused.

E) Motions can be made by any member of the club, but must be seconded. After it is seconded it will be discussed openly and then shall be voted on. (Simple majority needed)

RULES FOR ACCEPTANCE INTO BROWN IMAGE CAR CLUB

A) Person must be eighteen years old or older, positively no exceptions!

B) Must own his own car, which must have rims, (rockets, supremes, wires, cragers, etc.). Car must have nice paint job, (no prime or large dents). Car must be lowered or lifted!

C) Must be interested in making BROWN IMAGE a better club.

D) Must be able to attend meeting and club activities.

E) Shall pay membership fee of ten dollars and will pay the club its monthly dues of five dollars.

VOTING

A) Every member has the right to vote. All decisions and elections are decided by club vote.

B) Persons on probation do not have the right to vote or set motions.

TREASURY RULES

A) The elected treasurer is solely responsible for all club monies. The only exception is tardy fines.

B) He shall also be responsible for club's records and receipts.

-1-

The Brown Image Car Club Rules. *Courtesy of Henry Rodriguez.*

Chris Rodriguez was one such leader who learned the values of organizational structure and leadership in courses he had taken in high school. As Alex "Cabby" Flores affirmed, "Chris was way ahead of his time." He was responsible for organizing many of the events for the club and was the originator of the idea of acquiring and establishing a clubhouse

The Brown Image Clubhouse, which sponsored many block parties. *Courtesy of Richie Burgos.*

A dance ticket sales check list shows one of the many ways in which Brown Image Car Club organized its activities. *Courtesy of Henry Rodriguez.*

in the 1970s. The clubhouse provided a convenient place in Logan Heights for Brown Image to gather and build community. This, among several other community-oriented activities, made Brown Image very popular and well known throughout the community for organizing dances and block parties. A notable aspect of the dances organized by Brown Image was its success in securing venues at Balboa Park, which was unprecedented at the time. These dances were supported by the City of San Diego and featured entertainment headliners such as the Midnighters from East Los Angeles, the most popular group at the time. It reaffirmed this sense of the brotherhood and the importance of culture at a historical moment of great ethnic pride and solidarity for Mexican Americans, as seen with other car clubs. This was embodied in the name of the club. It integrated ethnic identity with lowriding. Brown Image sponsored numerous events throughout San Diego, inviting popular groups to perform.

Brown Image Car Club became so popular that San Diego law enforcement and the Mayor's Office found themselves facing challenges from

The Brown Image baseball team poses for a picture in Chicano Park. *Courtesy of Henry Rodriguez.*

A poster for the first annual Day in the Park, held in 1979. *Courtesy of Henry Rodriguez.*

the lowriding and Logan Heights community and eventually putting forth a public apology after the Northern Division of the San Diego Police Department unjustifiably entered the Brown Image clubhouse in 1975 in an early morning

54

raid without explanation. Chief of Police Bill Kolender and Mayor Pete Wilson apologized the following day and made a promise to the community that such an incident would never happen again. For many, this activity by law enforcement was seen as a strategy to break up the club because it was becoming "too big and popular," according to Henry Rodriguez. A few years later, Brown Image would be at the forefront of organizing "Day at the Park," an event for all lowrider car clubs from throughout San Diego to come to Chicano Park for a region-wide event celebrating the lowrider community and addressing the challenges it faced, such as achieving respectability and support for its activities—especially from the local police. In retrospect, we can assert that Brown Image Car Club was the first car club to actively engage law enforcement. The club was a force to contend with, particularly given that under Chris's leadership, it did everything by the book and was done exceptionally well. Members' hard work made an impression and over time has left quite an imprint on the community. As a result, they found themselves defenders of the community, and people looked to them to lead and provide support.

It is important to note the role of women in the history of Brown Image. Benita Perez, Ivy Westmoreland, Lydia Flores, Rebecca Nodal, Virginia Pacheco, Mona Cervantes, Janine Lopez-Rodriguez, Connie Cardenas, Juli Alvarado, Bebe Egipto and Helen Juarez were integral parts of the car club, and their unwavering support for the club is a story that has yet to be told. They supported the car club from the beginning and need to be acknowledged for their contributions and leadership.

The early lowrider car-hopping in the beginning of the 1970s by Brown Image Car Club. *Courtesy of Henry Rodriguez.*

Close-up of
the back of the
Brown Image
letterman car
club jacket.
*Courtesy of Henry
Rodriguez.*

Brown Image was one of the first car clubs to introduce street car-hopping,
where cars compete to see which car can hop the highest. Brown Image
was one of the first clubs to utilize hydraulics in a competitive way. It was
all about the competition and who could achieve bragging rights for being
the "best hopper" in San Diego. (See Street Vistas on page 62 to learn more
about hydraulics in the history of the lowrider movement.) Club members
experimented with their hydraulic setup and learned they could drop their
cars to create sparks that would emerge from the back of their car as it was
dropped. This is how Juan Rangel acquired the name "Johnny Flames." Chris
Rodriguez was known throughout San Diego as an impressive hopper and was
challenged by numerous other car clubs whose members owned vehicles with
newly acquired hydraulic systems. It represented a new edition to lowrider street
culture. In many ways, Brown Image set the standard for lowriding. As with
the early car clubs, club members' vehicles had remarkable paint jobs and car
customizing. Around 1976, the club began to lose members, who needed to
support their families, and continued to feel the pressure of law enforcement
constraints. These factors brought the club to an end. At present, the early
members of Brown Image have been meeting and plan to reestablish their
participation in the San Diego lowrider scene.

Regents Car Club of Sherman Heights and Logan Heights

In 1971, several young San Diego High School students from Sherman Heights and neighboring Logan Heights found themselves swept up into the lowrider explosion and were eager to make their mark on the lowrider scene. As with so many other car enthusiasts from this era, they admired and respected the Brown Image Car Club; however, Brown Image had an age restriction, and these guys were too young. So they responded by saying, "The heck with this—we'll establish our own club!" As a result, the Regents Car Club was born. Founding members were Carlos Vasquez, Rolando Mazon, Elias Gutierrez, Mundo Villa, Tommy Hinojosa, Robert Marquez, Alex Flores, Eddie Galindo, Johnny Hernandez, Robert Maestres and Gino

Regents Car Club founding member Carlos Vasquez poses with his car club jacket. *Courtesy of Keily Becerra.*

This lowrider was owned by Rolando Mazon of Regents Car Club. *Courtesy of Rolando Mazon.*

This 1968 Chevy Caprice was owned by Rolando Mazon of Regents Car Club. *Courtesy of Rolando Mazon.*

Vicaldo. They had several hangout spots, including Rolando Mazon's house in front of Sherman Elementary school. Amazingly enough, most of the members had vehicles. The club's name came from Tommy Hinojosa, who was college bound and knew the title for members of the governing board of the University of California was a regent. Hinojosa advocated for this name because he felt it would give them a great deal of status as an up-and-coming lowrider car club. The club members liked to paint and build cars, and as we have seen in so many of the other car clubs, although they had limited resources, their creativity, resourcefulness and ingenuity prevailed in their customization work. They created some elegant and impressive lowriders. As the club evolved, it had youth coming together from both the communities of Sherman Heights and Logan Heights. By around 1973, members of the club would get involved in new things, and some would move into becoming part of a new car club known as New Wave.

CLASSICS CAR CLUB OF OTAY

At the age of sixteen, Jesús "Chacho" Amezcua relocated to the small community of Otay from the city of Santa Ana, California. He enrolled at Castle Park High School in the neighboring city of Chula Vista, where he soon learned about Los Aztecas Car Club. The Aztecas were best known as a "high riders" car club, and members spent their time racing in Tijuana and Tecate, Mexico. As Chacho stated, the club was into *quemando llanta*, or "burning rubber." Chacho had a different style, having been a "backseat lowrider cruiser" back in Santa Ana. But he had arrived to south San Diego with his 1964 Chevy Impala Super Sport ready to cruise. Hence, he convinced his friends to "bounce" and create an exclusive lowrider car club. After a group vote, they became the Classic Car Club of Otay in 1971. Chacho had a cousin who was a member of the Classic Car Club of Santa Ana, and he asked for permission to borrow the name, not knowing they would endure over the years. After a few years, the club dropped the community reference to Otay to avoid turf conflicts and challenges with other members living in the Otay community. Along with Chacho, founding members were Moises Banuelos, Willie Gutierrez, Josue Aguilar, Jorge Flores, Arturo Vizaracho, Joe Muñoz, David Guzman, Joe Baldivia and Luis Cordero.

During this period, club members had nice cars because everyone had good-paying jobs. They could afford to customize and personalize their

A group shot of Classics Car Club. *Courtesy of Ernie Carrillo.*

A Classics Car Club jacket draped on the steering wheel. *Courtesy of Chacho Amezcua.*

vehicles. Sal Gallegos's 1947 Chevy Fleetmaster was a great example of the lowrider cars that were created during this period. Gallegos's vehicle embodied that classic '70s lowrider style discussed earlier in this chapter. Here was a car with show pipes, visible chrome throughout and a customized interior, in addition to being lifted with hydraulics. The Fleetmaster had been painted with polyurethane paint mixed with a ground metallic, making it virtually chip-resistant. Polyurethane paint had just become available and was used by some lowriders. What is important to note is that all of this customizing had been incorporated into an older classic vehicle. This trend was first introduced by the Latin Lowrider Car Club and continued throughout this era, culminating with Classic Car Club. Whereas some club members introduced newer cars into the lowrider car scene throughout this era, much of the car customizing was displayed on older, more classic vehicles. Consider Latin Lowriders with Henry Lozano's 1954 Chevy "Betzylu" and Richie Burgos's 1952 Chevy sedan, Brown Image's 1958 Impala belonging to Jesse Rios and Chicano Brothers' 1950 Chevy Fleetline owned by David Aguilar. Economics was part of the reason car club members chose older cars over newer ones. In addition, there was always a strong work ethic within the lowrider car customizing scene and a high value placed on crafting and building a car from scratch, personalizing it and truly making it your own creation.

Classics Car Club always focused on doing good for the larger community. Much of its vision was to have the community endorse and support its activities. In addition to its annual Otay Lakes picnic, open to all car clubs, Classics Car Club organized fundraisers for nonprofit organizations such as ARC of San Diego, which provides assistance to disabled adults. Like with several other car clubs in the San Diego lowrider world, Classics Car Club became known for its community service. The club has many good memories of hanging out at the Shell gas station on the corner of Third Avenue and Palomar Street in Chula Vista with permission from the owner. It was a welcoming space for all lowrider car clubs.

As Classic Car Club began to grow and evolve throughout the 1970s, issues of respect and self-discipline became topics in the lowrider community in San Diego with the advent of negative media portrayals and stereotypes of the lowrider lifestyle and culture like in the film *Boulevard Nights*. The film, directed by Michael Pressman, was responsible for lowrider car clubs having to defend themselves against the atrocious and erroneous depiction of lowriders as gangbangers. As heard from all of the lowrider clubs throughout San Diego, no one would be stupid

Street Vistas

HYDRAULICS AND THE LOWRIDER MOVEMENT

Car hydraulics are mechanical devices that make a car go up or down. Ron Aguirre from San Bernardino, California, was the first person to use hydraulic Pesco pumps in 1956. The first hydraulics to come onto the San Diego lowrider scene were recycled airplane landing gear purchased from Palley's Supply Company in Los Angeles during the 1960s. After acquiring such parts, the lowriders used their Chicano ingenuity to quickly figure out how to adapt and customize such devices onto their vehicles. Some community members took gate lifts designed for trucks and adapted and customized them to their cars. Limited resources made the lowrider community deeply resourceful and imaginative.

The advent of car hydraulics in the lowrider scene was a direct response to law enforcement, who actively ticketed vehicles for being too low to the ground. Hydraulic systems in lowriders allowed owners to be in full control of their vehicles despite crackdowns by authorities seeking to curtail cruising. Historically, hydraulics are a status symbol within the larger custom car world; they are a distinguishing factor of the lowrider community, giving it strength and a unique identity. There is something to be said about a car that can be both lowered and raised within seconds. You can make your car look different in an instant. The commercialization of hydraulics has resulted in the ability for anyone to go online and buy entire kits from custom shops that specialize in installing and adapting them to your vehicle. That

Korner Car Club car-hopping activities. *Courtesy of George Rodriguez.*

Chicano ingenuity that characterizes the community has been lost in the process. In addition, "air bags" or an air ride suspension, have replaced the more tedious and complicated mechanical hydraulic system for raising and lowering a vehicle, though this method is considered controversial by established lowriders.

enough to invest thousands of dollars into their vehicles—transforming them into their pride and joy—and then engage in risky behavior that would jeopardize their investment and their personal statement embodied in their customized car. A major outcome from these negative depictions was the creation and establishment of the San Diego Lowrider Council, which organized the lowrider community to defend itself and speak in a collective voice. We elaborate on this vision of respectability in the chapters that follow.

The foundational era in San Diego lowrider history is marked by the emergence of exclusively lowrider car clubs. A style all its own that today is referred to as that '70s classic lowrider vehicle is discussed throughout this chapter. This period establishes some key car aesthetics and styles that persist in the present-day lowrider world. It set the foundation for a developmental era when lowriding would be affirmed and sustained, taking us back to south San Diego communities and crossing the U.S.-Mexico border to the *colonias* of Tijuana.

3

The Affirming of Lowrider Identity in San Diego and Tijuana, 1972-74

D uring the brief period covered in this chapter, the lowriding style that began in the foundational era (described in chapter 2) further developed and became a more distinct style of customization. We begin with a club from south San Diego and then return to the heart of San Diego to discuss a club that embodies the lowrider identity. This identity is examined in relation to the trend of introducing new, elegant cars into the San Diego lowrider scene. We also learn about another young lowrider car club that would represent the next generation of lowriding. Finally, this chapter includes the perspective of a key lowrider car club born in Colonia Cortines in Tijuana, Mexico.

Casinos Car Club of San Ysidro

In the late 1960s, it was decided by Sweetwater Unified District that all students graduating from Southwest Junior High would have to attend Mar Vista High School in the neighboring town of Imperial Beach because their community had no high school for them to attend. Five young men from San Ysidro—Edwardo Corona, Miguel Croce, Jose Meza, Roberto Unibe and Placido Villareal—were all ninth graders and directly affected by this decision. They would embark on the daily three- to five-mile trek instead of waiting for the school bus to transport them from San Ysidro to Imperial

Mathias Ponce poses with the Serra Car Club plaque. *Courtesy of Alberto Pulido.*

Though initially known for his work on lowriding, Mathias Ponce took on drag racing. He is known in the world of drag racing as *el Águila*, or "the Eagle." *Courtesy of Mathias Ponce.*

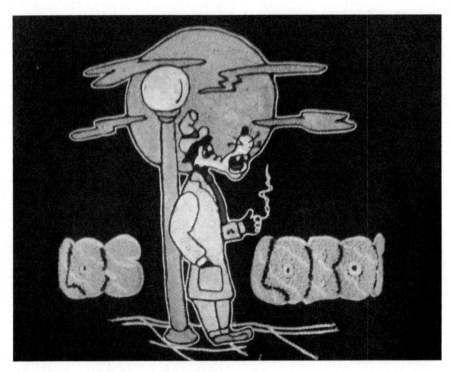

The original Los Lobos Jacket Club. *Courtesy of Alberto Pulido.*

Los Villanos Car Club jacket. *Courtesy of Marivn Israel Berechyahu Mayorga.*

The original
Coachmen
Car Club
sweatshirt.
*Courtesy of
Alberto Pulido.*

Luis "Louie" Sanchez (*left*) and Javier Ramirez (*right*), founding members of Baja Kings, pose with the original Baja Kings plaque. *Courtesy of Keily Becerra.*

The 1973 Montego also known as "Montezuma's Revenge," owned by Javier Fierro of Latin Lowriders Car Club. *Courtesy of Richie Burgos.*

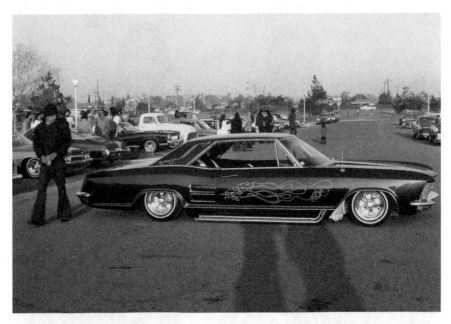

The 1964 Purple Riviera belonging to Richard Acosta of Latin Lowriders Car Club. *Courtesy of Richie Burgos.*

The 1952 Chevy sedan "Delivery" owned by Richie Burgos of Latin Lowriders Car Club. *Courtesy of Richie Burgos.*

David Aguilar's 1950 Chevy Fleetline. *Courtesy of David Aguilar.*

This 1966 Silver Impala belonged to Leo Hernandez of Chicano Brothers Car Club. The car was lifted and customized with rocket rims. *Courtesy of Leo Hernandez.*

This 1969 custom Buick Riviera belonged to Oscar Eribez of Brown Image Car Club. *Courtesy of Henry Rodriguez.*

This 1958 Impala with a chopped top belonged to Jesse Rios of Brown Image Car Club. *Courtesy of Henry Rodriguez.*

The original members Rolando Mazón and Carlos Vasquez of Regents Car Club pose today with their car club jackets. *Courtesy of Keily Becerra.*

The 1947 Chevy Fleetmaster owned by Sal Gallegos of Classics Car Club. *Courtesy of Chacho Amezcua.*

Willie Estrada of United Browns Car Club poses alongside his 1968 Chevy Impala in Tijuana. *Courtesy of Willie Estrada.*

This 1973 Buick Riviera, owned by Rolando Mazón, reflects the style of luxury vehicles owned by New Wave Car Club. *Courtesy of Rolando Mazón.*

One example of Korner Car Club's annual car-hops at the San Diego County Administration Building. *Courtesy of George Rodriguez.*

A street shot of the Domestic Rides Car Club. *Courtesy of Larry Flores.*

The 1959 Chevy Impala known as "Azteca" was owned by Rigoberto Reyes of Amigos Car Club. *Courtesy of Rigo Reyes.*

A close-up of the art on "Azteca," owned by Rigoberto Reyes. *Courtesy of Rigo Reyes.*

This 1977 Ford LTD belonged to Arturo Herrera of Amigos Car Club. *Courtesy of Arturo Herrera.*

The artwork on Manuel "Meño" Careño's 1978 Ford Ranchero. *Courtesy of Meño Careño.*

This 1978 Monte Carlo was owned by Elsa Castillo from Ladies Pride Car Club. *Courtesy of Elsa Castillo.*

Members of Specials Car Club during a get-together. *Courtesy of Diana Gonzalez.*

Back view of a 1978 Ford Thunderbird owned by Allen "Butch" Sherman of Groupe Car Club. *Courtesy of Allen "Butch" Sherman.*

Victor "Buzz" Muñoz poses in front of his 1964 Buick Riviera as a member of Casinos Car Club, 1976. *Courtesy of Rigo Reyes.*

Muñoz painted his 1964 Buick Riviera after joining the Amigos Car Club. It was given the name Pink Panther. *Courtesy of Rigo Reyes.*

The Pink Panther was sold to Steve "Masa" Wade, who transformed it into "Beyond Imagination" during the 1980s. *Courtesy of Steve "Masa" Wade.*

Jaime Machorro purchased Beyond Imagination from Steve and then sold it to the late Gaspar "Grandpa" Martinez. After Gaspar's untimely passing, his brother Pablo Martinez took it to the next level of customization. Today it's known as "Timeless," in memory of Gaspar. *Courtesy of Rigo Reyes.*

A bride and groom ride in the back seat of a 1969 Chevy Impala owned by Benjamin Osorio of Unlimited Car Club. *Courtesy of Benjamin Osorio.*

The 1977 Chevy Monte Carlo "Purple Rain," owned by Alejandro Lemus of Individuals Car Club, photographed in 1991. *Courtesy of Armando Medina.*

The founding member of the Casinos Car Club (*from left to right*): Edwardo Corona, Jose Meza, Toby Martinez, Roberto Unibe and Placido Villareal. Member Miguel Croce not pictured. *Courtesy of Miguel Croce.*

Beach. They resented the fact that they had to wait for the bus, so they would find alternative transportation options to attend school. There were even times when Miguel would show up offering rides to his friends with a car that he acquired from his father, who was a mechanic in Tijuana living in Cañon Johnson. As Mexican kids from San Ysidro who had to attend a majority white school in Imperial Beach, these young men faced discrimination by the dominant population. Attempting to reduce conflicts and tension between the two groups, the high school segregated the two populations with morning and evening sessions. As Toby Martinez described, "Whites in the morning and Mexicans in the evenings." All of this was significant because it produced a tightknit community and led them to want to do more as a group. During these early years, these young men were more of a social club without cars and considered good kids by the elders in the community.

Casinos Car Club members at their hangout spot in San Ysidro. *Courtesy of Miguel Croce.*

A Spanish-language news article recognizes Casinos Car Club for its positive contribution to the community. *Courtesy of Miguel Croce.*

A group picture of Casinos Car Club of San Ysidro, California. *Courtesy of Edwardo Corona.*

Due to external pressures described in the previous chapter, they were very conscientious about being seen as upstanding members of the community and not troublemakers. They embraced their strong bond as a social club. As a result, the club partook in church bazaars and fundraising activities for the betterment of the community.

Over the years, these young men would share dreams and life goals, one of which was to own cars and begin a car club. As the guys became older, they eventually acquired cars, with Miguel's 1955 Chevy being the first. During the Fiestas Patrias to celebrate Mexican Independence at the Misión Del Sol in Tijuana around 1972, the club unveiled its new jackets, marking Casinos Car Club's official entry into the lowrider car scene.

It is important to underscore that the club spent a great deal of its time in Tijuana cruising Avenida Revolución and cosponsoring dances with many of the car clubs, in particular Los Vagabundos Car Club from La Zona Norte in Tijuana. Casinos Car Club was extremely active in raising monies for the orphanages in Tijuana and would spend entire days visiting with the children as they prepared meals for them and distributed gifts. The members recalled

This 1964 Buick Riviera was owned by Victor "Buzz" Muñoz of Casinos Car Club. *Courtesy of Rigo Reyes.*

The 1964 Buick Riviera "Timeless" is owned by Pablo Martinez. *Courtesy of Rigo Reyes.*

that such experiences were deeply emotional because of the vulnerability expressed by the kids but, in the end, were also deeply rewarding for them. Casinos Car Club raised funds for the Tijuana Fire Department in addition to assisting it with its own fundraising campaigns. By the mid-1970s, Casinos Car Club would go through some changes and became somewhat inactive. It was during this period that Edwardo introduced the remaining members to his cousin from Los Angeles who belonged to Amigos Car Club. He was very impressed with the good work that had come from Casinos Car Club and asked if they would be willing to represent Amigos Car Club as a San Diego chapter. There was much debate and conversation regarding this request, but by 1977, Casinos Car Club would transition into Amigos Car Club.

In 1976, Casino Car Club member Victor "Buzz" Muñoz purchased a 1964 Buick Rivera from Gerardo "Jerry" Sevilla from Brown Image. Victor felt proud of this car, and one of the first things he did was add blue side panels. Soon after Casinos became Amigos, Victor was inspired to paint the Rivera a tangerine color mixed with pearl undertones. To his surprise, instead of the tangerine he envisioned, the paint dried pink. When club members saw this alteration, they quickly baptized his vehicle "Pink Panther." The third transformation of this vehicle was into "Beyond Imagination" in 1985 by Steve "Masa" Wade. The most recent modification, into "Timeless," began in 2000 by Pablo Martinez and continues into the present. We have chosen to feature this 1964 Buick Rivera to highlight the significance of car customization in the lowrider community. It speaks to the importance and value of a vehicle over time.

United Browns Car Club of Tijuana, Mexico

With guidance from his brother Roberto Estrada and friend Toño Gallardo, Guillermo "Willie" Estrada decided to change his cruising style from a "high-rider" to a lowrider in 1974. Living in Colonia Cortines, he got involved with the Tijuana car club known as United Brown, which had begun in 1972. Willie *tumbó* (lowered) his 1968 Chevrolet Impala, added white-wall tires and became a full-fledged member of United Browns Car Club.

Recognizing the rich and important history of lowriding in Tijuana and other Mexican border communities with car clubs such as Los Dukes, Los Knights, Los Yoguis, we focus on United Browns in this book because it was the first car club to emerge exclusively as a lowrider car club. Similar

Members from the United Browns Car Club from Tijuana. *Courtesy of Willie Estrada.*

An invitation to all San Diego lowrider car clubs for an event organized and hosted by the United Browns Car Club of Tijuana. *Courtesy of Willie Estrada.*

A member from United Browns Car Club from Tijuana poses with a member from Latin Lowriders of San Diego at a 1976 reception in Tijuana. *Courtesy of Willie Estrada.*

to the early lowrider movement in San Diego, the majority of early Tijuana lowrider car clubs had a mixture of customized lowriders and hot rods. In addition, many of the car clubs in Tijuana are *clubs automovilísticos*, or "automobile clubs," that are recognized as a civic organization by the municipal government. These automobile clubs also offer a great deal of social services to the larger community.

United Browns had around fifteen members and would meet regularly at El Arizona, a Chinese restaurant on the corner of Agua Calientes and Ocampo Boulevards in Tijuana. These meetings would be followed by a cruise, referred to as a *rondín*, down to Playas de Tijuana, designated as the cruising spot in Tijuana. Lowriders would also spend time at *el malecón*, or "the seafront," which was a very popular hangout spot. Their evenings would end at the Aloha Night Club, located on the famous Avenida Revolución, which drew in hundreds of patrons on a weekly basis. As a lowrider car club, United Brown was very conscientious about appearance and dress of its members. As an exclusively Tijuana car club, members were critical of the appearance of Chicano lowrider car clubs from San Diego and had been influenced by the negative depictions of Chicano lowriders popular in the U.S. mainstream media to discredit the lowrider lifestyle.

Nonetheless, camaraderie existed between the San Diego and Tijuana clubs. The United Browns sponsored San Diego car clubs, such as the Latin Lowriders. This act of *compadrazgo* went a long way in validating and affirming San Diego lowriders, who were not always accepted by the San Diego community. It was very common for the early Chicano car clubs to have sponsorship and to be invited to cruise with the Tijuana car clubs at Playas as well as attend their numerous dances at El Club Campestre or El Salón Nicte-Ha. There is such a deep and rich history of Tijuana lowriding that it requires a book of its own. We simply wish to introduce the topic but highly encourage more historical research on this significant subject.

NEW WAVE CAR CLUB OF SHERMAN HEIGHTS AND ENCANTO

By the early 1970s, some lowriders found themselves wishing to continue the tradition but were without a car club. This was the case for Jesse "Bird" Lopez, Pico Rivera, Rolando Mazon and Michael Ortega. One had been with the Latin Lowriders and another with Regents Car Club, and all had

Some members from New Wave Car Club from Sherman Heights and Encanto. *Courtesy of Rolando Mazon.*

An invitation for an event hosted by New Wave Car Club. *Courtesy of Rolando Mazon.*

This early 1970s Ford Thunderbird belonged to Jesse Flores from New Wave Car Club. *Courtesy of Rolando Mazon.*

This early 1970s Buick Riviera belonged to Rolando Mazon from New Wave Car Club. *Courtesy of Rolando Mazon.*

This early 1970s Buick Riviera, belonging to Rolando Mazon, reflects the type of vehicles used by New Wave Car Club. *Courtesy of Rolando Mazon.*

been influenced by Brown Image. Through Lopez, the group learned that New Wave Car Club of Los Angeles had broken up. The guys liked the name, so they decided to use it and come out as a new San Diego Lowrider Car Club in 1973. As the name depicts, the club wanted to emphasize something different—a new style that you could see by their choice of vehicles.

As a result, the car club focused on customizing and showcasing new cars that were elegant and beautiful. We should not lose sight that the 1970s was an era of transition, and people were open to all that was new and fresh. As Rolando Mazon remarked, this was a period of many opportunities and "open windows." Two notable vehicles from this club was Rolando Mazon's Riviera and Jesse Flores's Thunderbird. These cars' style made New Wave well known through San Diego.

It also helped that the club held popular picnics, dances and battle of the band events at Morley Field and Crowne Point in San Diego. It organized many activities at Chicano Park, where it also held its initial club meetings. Another very popular place to gather during this period was the Otto Square Shopping Center located in Southeast San Diego. All the activities organized by New Wave Car Club were done with the idea to help support the community. Like so many other car clubs, this is why its members did the work and came together.

The New Wave Logo. *Courtesy of Rolando Mazon.*

By the mid-1970s, the club had begun to spend more time in National City and lay claim to being one of the first clubs to ignite the cruising scene on Highland Avenue. Other car clubs like Latin Lowriders would hang out near Highland, but New Wave actually began the cruise in search of dates and good times and to check out the new cars. The group established a clubhouse at the home of Joe Paniagua in National City and cruised the boulevard every weekend. The inception of cruising Highland Avenue is critically important to the lowrider life style during this era and beyond. With all of the complications and conflicts that ensued among communities, lowrider car clubs and law enforcement, Highland Avenue represents the mecca of the lowrider car scene in San Diego during the 1970s. It endowed lowriding with a character and identity. The importance of Highland is discussed in the "Street Vistas" offered in chapter 4.

As club members began to marry, join the service and get involved in new things, the club began to slow down and was disbanded by 1978. Soon after, others came along and reignited New Wave. By around 1980, the club was back together and on the streets. At present, New Wave Car Club is very active, represented by members from throughout San Diego with many stunning cars. The club continues to hold its meeting at Chicano Park, and this new phase of New Wave represents the next generation of lowriders.

Klique Car Club of Southeast San Diego

Klique Car Club emerged on the lowrider scene in San Diego around 1974. Brothers Pepe and Paco Alvarado, Loretto "Lonely" Romero, "Negris" Romero, Chuy Soto, Frank Sandoval, Bobby Covarrubias and "Night-Owl" are some of its founding members. Some of these individuals had come from Brown Image Car Club and were seeking new opportunities and expressions in the lowrider community. They agreed that they would travel to East Los Angeles and meet with the founding chapter of Klique, requesting permission to begin a chapter in San Diego. They were successful and were an active car club up until 1981. Two years later, in 1983, the car club was brought back to life. Jesús "Chato" Esparza and Oscar "Fat Rat" Mendez began talking and planning on how to get Klique started up again. Their biggest challenge was they lacked experience on how to go about doing this. Coincidently, brothers Adolfo and Ernie Martinez, along with Richard "Drac" Rodriguez, had similar sentiments. Adolfo happen to own an auto body and paint shop, and Chato just happened to be in need

The Klique Car Club in 1980. *Courtesy of Carol Raymond.*

of painting his 1976 Caprice Classic. So he went to go see Adolfo, and as they say, the rest is history. Chato and Adolfo put their heads together to bring forth a new chapter of Klique Car Club. Klique was always active at the annual Chicano Park Day in San Diego, not to mention consistently organized picnics and toy drives, and was active in softball tournaments. By the late 1980s, Klique was very involved with the San Diego Lowrider Council through the leadership of Carlos Contreras, who had become club president. One of Carlos's proudest accomplishments was playing a part in coordinating the mural at Chicano Park dedicated to the San Diego Lowrider Council that features a variety of lowriders, including his 1964 ragtop. The mural was completed in 2007. Klique remains a very strong car club with thirty members. It continues to host numerous family-oriented events. Several of the members are building and creating car show–quality vehicles. The car club is now based in Logan Heights.

CUSTOM CAR CLUB OF NATIONAL CITY

A group of young men from National City Junior High School were swept up into the lowrider car scene as a result of their elder brothers, who owned lowriders and were actively cruising the streets of National City. In 1974, Frank Jaime, Dave Diaz, Eddie Macias, Andrew Camacho, George Arce, Eddie "Shark" Gonzalez, "Jaybird" Galvan, "Jimbo" Davis, Steve Contreras, David Gomez and Johnny Sontoya were excited about creating a lowrider car club despite the fact that none of them possessed a driver's license. Yet the excitement generated by hanging out with their brothers and learning about the lowrider way of life led Andrew Camacho and Dave Diaz to design the first plaque for Custom Car Club of National City despite the fact that none of the members owned vehicles. Within a few years, these committed young men would follow in their brothers' footsteps, acquire and customize cars and fully enter the lowrider car scene in National City. Club members owned fully customized cars that emphasized the ingenuity of these young Chicanos. Frank Jaime's 1969 Ford LTD, David Diaz's Ford Galaxy 500, Jimbo Davis's Cutlass Supreme and Steve Contreras's '74 Chevy Monte Carlo stood out as some of their best lowrider vehicles.

Custom Car Club would gather on Friday nights at the home of president Frank Jaime, who lived on Twenty-Second Street, right behind the Mile of Cars in National City. It was part of the club's tradition to go check

The original members of the Customs Car Club of National City, California. *Courtesy of Carol Raymond.*

out the scene by cruising nearby Highland Avenue. The club was known for its weekly football and baseball tournaments between the car clubs that occurred at Sweetwater High School. Customs was also active in the San Diego Lowrider Council. A few years back, the club began to fade, but it is being brought back into the contemporary lowrider scene by one of its founding member, Dave Diaz.

Street Vistas

THE LOWRIDER CAR CLUB COUNCIL OF SAN DIEGO, CALIFORNIA

The San Diego Lowrider Car Club Council was established in 1979 with the mission to promote a positive image of lowriders and barrios in San Diego. In preparation for the ninth anniversary of Chicano Park, hosted by Latin Lowriders, a meeting was organized to discuss one of the first organized car exhibitions at the park. The idea was fostered at that meeting, and the council was established. Brown Image, Classics, Korner, New Wave, Customs, Oldies and Amigos were among the first clubs to participate. Over the years, some of the car clubs had been part of conflicts stemming from community rivalries and turf battles. The council emerged as a forum for negotiating differences and long-standing conflicts and as a welcoming space for all with an eye toward coordinating citywide events. The council stopped meeting around 1983, when the majority of the older car clubs started to disband. In 1985, it was reestablished as the San Diego Lowrider Council.

At present, there are about eleven car clubs, although previously the council had up to sixteen car clubs. The council is the oldest active car coalition in the country. San Diego lowriders are recognized as being among the more organized, having run a successful boycott against Lowrider Magazine Car Show in 2002 because of the treatment of the participants and the cost to enter the show. Annual Chicano Park Day celebrations bring top-quality

San Diego Lowrider Council, established in 1979, brought together all lowrider car clubs from throughout San Diego, as evident in this 1989 photograph. *Courtesy Raul Rodriguez.*

car show vehicles for viewing, free to the general public. The San Diego Lowrider Car Council continues to be the main source of information, coordination and communication within the lowrider community.

Biography and history have a lot to do with the characteristics of the various lowrider car clubs in San Diego. Each car club described in this chapter offers its own distinctive features because of the biography of each club member, his history and the place where he experienced and learned about lowriding. The history of San Diego lowriding provides an exclusive perspective because, as illustrated in this chapter, lowriding in the borderlands crosses borders, bringing out qualities and expressions that can be found only in this part of the world.

4

The Old and the New

Car-Hopping, Blessings and the Legacy of Lowriding, 1975-77

This chapter introduces more car clubs that are customizing and lowering new cars alongside a club that emphasizes older cars, or *ranflas*. In this chapter, we underscore the tenacity of traditional lowriding as revealed through organized car-hops and the essential values of lowrider legacies in terms of building community through relationships and upholding the history of the lowrider movement.

Oldies Car Club of Logan Heights

Oldies Car Club began in the summer of 1975. During a lunch break at the local shipyard, two workers, Joe Navarez and Jesse Alvarado, came up with the idea of starting up a lowrider car club made up of strictly old vehicles. They put together a flyer announcing this idea, distributed it widely and asked for folks to come to Chicano Park on July 10 if they were interested. To their surprise, eighteen clean *ranflas* from throughout San Diego showed up, and by the end of the meeting, Oldies Car Club had formed with ten members. Members began to debate and discuss the name of the club, and Eddie Galindo brought up the idea that they should be called the Oldies Car Club since Oldies was the style of music they listened to and the type of cars they owned and cruised. As a family-oriented car club, Oldies attracted new members. In 1981, club

The Oldies Car Club in 1980. *Courtesy of Carol Raymond.*

members became aware of an Oldies Car Club in the San Fernando Valley and contacted the club. They invited Oldies San Fernando to Chicano Park Day in 1981. Upon meeting and spending time together, both clubs realized that they shared common interests in their love and respect for old vehicles and their desire to unite the brotherhood within the lowrider community throughout the Southwest region, described as *Aztlán* by many from the Chicano lowrider community. In 1983, the San Fernando chapter of Oldies disbanded to join the Dukes Car Club of Los Angeles. By 1986, some of the ex-members of Oldies from the San Fernando chapter joined up with Oldies of San Diego.

Two of the most notable cars from Oldies Car Club are Beto Zamasa's 1948 Plymouth, back in the early days of the club, and Robert Carrillo's 1954 Chevy. Oldies has been active with the annual caravans of Our Lady of Guadalupe Church in Logan Heights in addition to participating in toy drives for children that led the group to launch a toy drive picnic in 1988 for a needy orphanage. This annual event was held from 1988 to 1999. Oldies Car Club is currently structured without a club president. The car club does have a sergeant at arms, a secretary and a treasurer. All active members have an equal vote, and all decisions are based on majority vote. There are currently nine chapters of Oldies Car Club throughout the American Southwest. Oldies has a high regard for a sense of collective unity through its members' love for cars alongside a strong commitment to represent and

The Oldies Car Club at the annual Lowrider Council picnic in 2016. *Courtesy of Marvin Israel Berechyahu Mayorga.*

highlight the lowrider scene through their support of Oldies vehicles on the streets of San Diego and throughout the Southwest.

There remains an active conversation within the San Diego lowrider community as to the establishment of Oldies Car Club between the years 1975 and 1978. As with all the other car clubs interviewed for this book, we honor the date put forth by the representatives of Oldies Car Club and report it as it was told to us.

KORNER CAR CLUB OF SHERMAN HEIGHTS

It was tradition for the "guys from the corner" to hang out, says George Rodriguez, founding member of Korner Car Club. It was the 1970s, and the corner was Island and Twenty-First Streets in San Diego. These were guys from throughout San Diego who simply liked to hang out. The gatherings became so common that the guys decided to start a social club with the name of Korner. As members got older and began to own cars, they decided that Korner should become a car club, and as a result Korner Car Club was born

Several Korner Car Club members in Chicano Park during an annual celebration of the blessing of the cars. *Courtesy of George Rodriguez.*

in 1977. In addition to George, some of the founding members included Lalo Delgadillo and Pablo Rios. Members of the club had learned about hydraulics and were eager to showcase them in a big way. Brown Image had started the tradition of car-hopping a few years prior, and members of Korner had learned about car-hops in Los Angeles. So Korner was excited to initiate an organized and competitive car-hop beginning in 1977.

What started off as a cool idea really took off and became popular with the lowrider community of San Diego. In fact, lowrider car clubs from Los Angeles began to compete against San Diego lowrider car clubs at the height of the annual car-hops sponsored by Korner Car Club. The competition was based on "one-pump hopping" to see which car could hop the highest. Korner actually used a wooden ruler to measure heights and determine the winner. Korner's car-hops ran annually from 1977 through 1985. During this era, it became a popular event alongside cruising Highland Avenue and gathering at Chicano Park. The majority of the fundraising activities organized by Korner, such as dances and car washes, was to raise funds and support the annual car-hop competition.

With the exception of one year, all of the car-hop competitions were held in the large parking lot of the San Diego County Administration building.

George Rodriguez of Korner Car Club and his Gran Torino in front of one of the monumental murals in Chicano Park during the annual blessing of the cars celebration. *Courtesy of George Rodriguez.*

This location is notable because it shows the role of the San Diego Police Department in assisting the lowrider community. Namely, Ernie Salgado and George Varela worked closely with Korner Car Club to secure the county parking lot on an annual basis. Along with these two gentlemen, other car clubs spoke highly of the support and assistance they received from George Saldamando from the San Diego Police Department. The

This 1947 Chevy Coupe is being blessed at Our Lady of Guadalupe Church in Logan Heights. *Courtesy of San Diego History Center.*

relationship between the police and lowrider community in the history of San Diego is mixed with positive and negative encounters. We learned about police harassment toward lowriders alongside moments of cooperation and support from the San Diego Police Department. Take, for example, the early morning raid of Brown Image Club House described in chapter 3, as well as the systematic shutting down of Highland Avenue by National City Police Department in the following chapters. But even as these events occurred, law enforcement supported various lowrider activities, such as the bike repair clinic organized by Nosotros Car Club described in chapter 2. The history of lowrider-police relations is an important and complicated topic that needs additional research.

Among the many vehicles belonging to Korner Car Club were three Ford Gran Torinos owned by three different Korner Car Club members. All were from the 1970s and gave the club a unique attribute distinguishing it from all other San Diego lowrider car clubs.

Father Richard Brown joined the Roman Catholic community at Our Lady of Guadalupe Church in Logan Heights in 1968. He represents a religious institution to the thousands who grew up in the community and attended Our Lady of Guadalupe Church. Having grown up five houses down from the parish, George Rodriguez came to respect and appreciate Father Brown. Around 1979, Korner Car Club gathered and organized a "blessing of the cars" event that became popular within the larger lowrider community. It was a powerful idea that intersected the lowrider community and the church in a meaningful way. Car blessings became very popular in the lowriding community as a sign of respect for the community and fellow car club members. In fact, religion continues to play a significant role in the lives of many lowrider car clubs that define themselves as Christian, such as the Disciples Car Club and Chosen Few Car Club from San Diego.

CITY CAR CLUB OF SAN DIEGO

Growing up, Hector Eribez looked up to his elder brother, Oscar. Hector and his friends admired Oscar because he was an integral member of Brown Image Car Club during the 1970s. As Hector boasted, "We were very proud of Oscar because he was a part of Brown Image. He was very inspirational to all of us." As Oscar's younger brother, Hector got to hang out with Brown Image and came to learn a great deal about the culture and history of lowriding. He came

The City Car Club in 1980. *Courtesy of Carol Raymond.*

to know Teddy Egipto and Chris Rodriguez, who represented the heart of
Brown Image. In particular, Chris became a mentor to Hector, teaching him
a great deal, while Hector admired the way Chris modeled "steppin out of the
box" within the lowrider world of San Diego. Chris was an inspiration to Hector
and motivated him to do more because he witnessed how he was able to take a
beginning car club and transform it into a big car club to the point that Brown
Image was recognized and respected throughout Southern California. By 1976,
Brown Image began to go dormant, and much of the leadership that Hector
admired left. Keeping in mind all that he had been taught over the years, Hector
moved forward to establish City Car Club in 1977 with Billy Vicaldo and others
from both San Diego and Sweetwater High Schools. City Car Club was active

Many lowrider groups assembled to protest the shutting down of Highland Avenue. In this image, City Car Club is the first on the scene. *Courtesy of San Diego History Center.*

in organizing dances and related social gatherings. It organized one of the first indoor exclusively lowrider car shows at the Golden Hall Convention Center in the early 1980s. City Car Club was active cruising Highland Avenue and was part of the protest that challenged Highland Avenue's shutdown.

AMIGOS CAR CLUB OF SOUTH SAN DIEGO

As was introduced in the previous chapter, Casinos Car Club of San Ysidro was going through numerous transitions and was in search of a new identity and name at the end of 1976. There was a strong desire among some of the active members for the club to transition into a San Diego car club and not strictly as a San Ysidro car club, as it had been up to this point. In addition, there were conversations about diminishing the club's consistent presence and interaction with Tijuana and instead have the club branch out and be more active within the San Diego lowrider car scene. This was supported by members who were wanting to change the club's image into a San Diego lowrider car club inspired by the beliefs of *Chicanismo* at its core. In particular,

Some of the original members of Amigos Car Club. *Courtesy of Rigo Reyes.*

Rigoberto Reyes and Arturo Herrera had been swept up by the Chicano activism proclaimed by César Chávez, Herman Baca and the visionaries who led the Chicano Park takeover in Logan Heights, including Jose Gomez, Josie Talamantez, Tommie Camarillo, Ramón "Chunky" Sanchez and the San Diego chapter of the Brown Berets de Aztlán. Throughout these numerous deliberations, Edwardo Corona introduced the club to his cousin from Amigos Car Club of Los Angeles and shared with the group the car plaque. Upon their seeing it, the deal was sealed, and there was unanimous support for the club to become Amigos Car Club of San Diego in 1977. The founding members were Arturo "Zorro" Herrera, Toby Martinez, Rigoberto "Rigo" Reyes, David Gutierrez, Arcadio "RK" Mora, Victor "Buzz" Muñoz, Danny Arellano, Octavio Aceves, Jimmy "Rat" Lontayo, Gaspar "Grandpa" Martinez, Raul "Indio" Guerrero and Raymond Bravo.

Amigos Car Club held its weekly meetings on Friday nights at the Palm City Teen Post on the corner of Beyer Boulevard and Coronado in south San Diego. Members cruised Highland Avenue later in the evening and then returned to their initial meeting space. Amigos became known for Memo Holguin's Monte Carlo because it had one of the very first murals to appear on a lowrider in San Diego and also their Ford LTDs that came out in the late 1970s owned by Arturo "Zorro" Herrera and Toby Martinez. Another important vehicle from this era was the 1959 Chevy Impala named "Azteca" owned by Rigo Reyes that was also customized with a beautiful mural painted by the customizer known as Wells. In the previous chapter,

A back shot of "Azteca," the 1959 Chevy Impala owned by Rigoberto Reyes of Amigos Car Club. *Courtesy of Rigo Reyes.*

A close-up of the customized grill of this 1964 Buick Riviera, owned by Victor "Buzz" Muñoz as a member of Amigos Car Club, when it was transformed into the "Pink Panther." *Courtesy of Rigo Reyes.*

A back shot of a 1957 Chevy with suicide doors belonging to Rigoberto Reyes at Chicano Park. *Courtesy of Rigo Reyes.*

we introduced Victor "Buzz" Muñoz's 1964 Buick Rivi and described its transformation into the "Pink Panther" during the early years of the club. A major contribution by Amigos Car Club is its active role in organizing and sponsoring the annual lowrider show as part of Chicano Park Day. Amigos has been at the forefront of this work since 1983 and continues to coordinate the largest car show in the region that is free of charge.

Amigos Car Club has been in existence for close to forty years. At the core of the club's legacy is its emphasis on preserving lowrider history, culture and tradition. Club members take great pride in recognizing and respecting the "standards" of traditional lowriding passed down to them from the *veteranos* of the lowrider movement, especially regarding the basics for customizing a lowrider. In the words of Toby Martinez, all of this represents the "theory of lowriding" that must be preserved and passed down to the current and future members of the lowrider community in order to keep the movement alive. It is described as an intuitive feeling that "comes from the heart." A lowrider car club is like being part of a family, "a sense of belonging to something…no longer needing to wander," noted Arturo "Zorro" Herrera.

Street Vistas
EXPLOSION OF HIGHLAND AVENUE, 1975

It is impossible to talk about the history of lowriding without also talking about cruising. The unique qualities of lowriding outlined at the outset of this book speak about an independent spirit with no boundaries or restrictions that is fully embodied in cruising. The heart of the cruising scene, in the history of lowriding, was Highland Avenue in National City. A long and wide street with an impressive vista that ascends in certain parts and descends in others, it is a natural and attractive place for car cruising. In San Diego, Highland was that natural meeting place in the center of the lowrider region. People from south of San Diego could go north, and people from the north could go south. With several businesses located on Highland, car clubs could designate parking lots for gathering and hanging out. Of course, this was not always to the liking of the businesses, so they would call law enforcement in to dissuade such activity. Overt tension and conflict between lowriders and law enforcement was a common occurrence on Highland, not unlike Whitter Boulevard in Los Angeles or the Mission District in San Francisco. All these places were synonymous with lowriding in their respective communities. Cruising was a weekend activity that usually began at dusk on Friday and ended on Sunday evening. The peak of Highland Avenue cruising was between 1975 and 1981. Other critical cruising locations in San Diego were Chicano Park, Golden Hills Park, Sea Port Village, Balboa Park and Mission Bay. Cruising Highland was made illegal by law enforcement in the early 1980s. More detail is provided in chapter 6.

Highland Avenue in 1971. This street was considered the most popular cruising spot for all San Diego lowriders until it was shut down by law enforcement in the 1980s. *Courtesy of Special Collections and Archives. Geisel Library, University of California–San Diego.*

5

Made in the USA and Women Lowrider Car Clubs, 1978–79

Feelings of pride, or *sentimientos de orgullo*, discussed in the opening chapter are fundamental to the history of lowriding in San Diego and signify an important emphasis in this chapter. We begin with a lowrider car club that proclaims its identity by applying basic principles of Chicano culture while driving exclusively American-made cars. At another level, we trace a notable moment in lowrider history with women moving from passengers to drivers as they hit the streets driving their own cars and flying their own plaques with a sense of pride, independence and ownership unprecedented in the history of lowriding.

Domestic Rides Car Club of Southeast San Diego

Domestic Rides Car Club began in 1979 with its founding members Larry Flores, Joe Skubski, Gilbert Montoya and Ray Ramirez. They met weekly at Chicano Park to establish the focus and purpose of the club. The early months of the club were a time of change and adjustments, with Larry chosen as president of the club. At first, he was a bit reluctant to take on such a high-profile role, but over time, he recognized the importance of his contribution. Larry's leadership role has been solid, and he has remained president of the club over its thirty-eight-year existence. As with so many

Members Manuel Careño and Larry Flores of Domestic Rides Car Club pose with their plaque. *Courtesy of Alberto Pulido.*

other lowrider car clubs, the best way to describe Domestic Rides Car Club is as a family. There is a strong spirit of *compadrazgo* where many of the original members remain and have seen one another's kids grow up. A crucial characteristic of Domestic Rides Car Club are the people who compose it. The structure of the club is based on people who know how to get along. The club prides itself on having nice cars owned by good people who demonstrate the values of Chicano culture and lowriding as described in the introduction.

The name of the club says it all in terms of the type of vehicles that define the club. This means that all cars in the club are American-made cars. The club is populated with Fords and Chevys owned by good people. The vehicles that stand out for the club are the customized truck-cars owned by Manuel "Meño" Careño. In the past, Meño owned a 1978 Ford Ranchero with striking customized mural work. It speaks to Meño's love for lions because he is a Leo in the astrological calendar. Both the mural and choice of vehicle are very unique within the San Diego lowrider community. At present, he owns a 1959 Chevy El Camino. It is beautiful

Close-up of the mural on this 1978 Ford Ranchero owned by Manuel Careño from Domestic Rides Car Club. *Courtesy of Meño Careño.*

in terms of design and color and is extremely rare as a lowrider. Both of these sport truck vehicles represent the exclusive lowrider cars to come out of Domestic Rides Car Club.

As a person-focused car club, Domestic Rides sees one of its most important roles within the San Diego lowrider community to be that of supporter. The club is very active in the San Diego Lowrider Council, and the club makes it a point to support all events publicized through the council. It is all about building and supporting the lowrider community so it will endure over the years.

LADIES PRIDE CAR CLUB OF SOUTH SAN DIEGO

Chris Cano grew up in the lowriding culture of south San Diego dominated by her family and friends who were all men. Upon discovering that access into these clubs was prohibited to women, Chris took matters into her own hands and in 1979 started her own car club. The Ladies Pride Car Club came onto the San Diego lowrider car scene as the first women-only lowrider car club in the history of the movement. Founding members were Chris Cano, Laura Vera, Elsa Castillo and Sandra Ardilla. They

Members from the Ladies Pride Car Club pose with their car plaques. *Courtesy of Elsa Castillo.*

A ticket to a dance organized and hosted by Ladies Pride. *Courtesy of Elsa Castillo.*

Ladies Pride Car Club members at their hangout spot at Montgomery Ward department store before the cruise on Highland. *Courtesy of Elsa Castillo.*

were nineteen- and twenty-year-old women who were striving to better themselves by holding down jobs and attending college and not having to depend on their parents or boyfriends. As women who possessed their own cars with a distinct look and style, they were a symbol of independence. This meant that they "could be part of a male-dominated tradition, but could stand on [their] own in a leadership role where [they] expressed [their] love for lowrider cars and tradition," according to Elsa Castillo. She continued, "Men would repetitively ask us, 'Hey, is that dad's car or your boyfriend's car,' and we would proudly proclaim, 'No, this is my car. I own it!'" These women took great pride in their cars.

One of the most popular places for the club to hang out was in the parking lot of the Montgomery Ward department store on Highland Avenue. This spot was especially popular on days when everyone was cruising this historic avenue. On other days, the club would gather at Chicano Park or at the various homes of club members accompanied by home-cooked Mexican meals prepared by the members' moms who supported their efforts. Like the male clubs of this era, Ladies Pride Car

Members of Ladies Pride Car Club attend a Classics Car Club dance. *Courtesy of Elsa Castillo.*

Club was proud of their new cars that they had customized into lowriders. Chris Cano's 1979 Buick Riviera and Elsa Castillo's 1978 Monte Carlo are good illustrations of their cars. Elsa's Monte Carlo was cutting edge; it had T-Tops, which were in vogue at the time. Another feature that Elsa was quite proud of was her elaborate sound system, with the latest technology. As noted in one of our previous Street Vistas, music was an integral part of the lowrider experience.

At its peak, the club had close to fifteen members with a total of eight members who were very committed club members. The club sponsored many picnics, holiday fundraisers and dances. The women of Ladies Pride Car Club spent a lot of time putting together outfits for their events. The objective was to be sure that they looked "classy" and dressed up. Dressing up was a message to the dominant culture that the women could be lowriders and look sharp and respectable through their appearance. It affirmed the importance of their club and their role in the community. As the women grew older and started to get into serious relationships, the club began to slow down and ended around 1981.

Specials Car Club of South San Diego

Under the leadership of Jo Anna Samora-Harris, a small group of young women at Mar Vista High School in the city of Imperial Beach began gathering and exploring the idea of beginning an all-women lowrider car club. Jo Anna had been exposed to lowrider car culture through her brother-in-law, who was a member of New Wave Car Club. She fell in love with the cars, the music, the people and, of course, the cruising. But as she looked around, she noticed that there were no clubs for women, and she wanted to change that. By 1979, Specials Car Club came onto the cruising scene similar to Ladies Pride. Founding members included Lisa Kirker, Lupe Waters, Debbie Sheppard, Alma Delarosa, Diana Gonzalez, Paula Jordan, Elsa Garcia, Maria Rosas and Michelle Kirker. Many club members owned new cars, such as the Oldsmobile Cutlass Supreme, but the club was not exclusively for members who owned new cars. They were interested in bringing together women from throughout San Diego who had a love for the lowrider way of life. The club would meet at the McDonald's parking lot on Highland and then cruise the boulevard. Club members organized picnics, dances and car washes and were active members of the San Diego Lowrider Car Council, as was Ladies Pride. Specials Car Club would begin to slow down by 1983, as its members married and had new challenges in their lives.

A 1978 Oldsmobile Cutlass owned by Nonie Samano from Specials Car Club. *Courtesy of Diana Gonzalez.*

One of the biggest regrets expressed by all members in both all-women clubs was the decision to sell their lowriders once they were married and had children. They could not keep up the demands of being a mother and continuing the lowrider lifestyle. Some of the women wished they would have held on to their cars to keep the female lowrider spirit alive to share with their daughters and women in general. It was noted that the majority of men who married and had children were able to preserve their vehicles and remain active, unlike female lowriders. At present, there are new women's lowrider car clubs coming onto the streets attracting some of these women back into cruising and taking to the streets. Former Specials Car Club member Nonie Samano is cruising once again, and she proudly flies the flag of Unique Ladies Car Club of San Diego.

Street Vistas
MEN AND WOMEN LOWRIDING OVER THE GENERATIONS

A major discovery to emerge from the history of lowriding between the years 1950 and 1985 is that it was a lifestyle expressed overwhelmingly by youth that were of middle and high school age, Lowrider car clubs gave men a sense of place and belonging that, for a variety of reasons, they could not find in their homes with their families. In contrast for women, the lowrider car club was seen as an extension of their families. This marked distinction has changed over the years as the lowrider community has aged, and we now have a large segment of the lowrider community who are now parents and grandparents. Hence, it is very common today to see lowrider-sponsored events with car club members getting together with their children and grandchildren, presenting us with a new and changing image of lowriding. One unfailing value from within the lowrider community regardless of gender is the support and unity that exist, especially in time of need or crisis. This represents part of the eight qualities of lowriding described in the introduction.

6

From the Streets to the Car Show

The End of the Foundational Lowrider Era, 1980-85

A s we have alluded to throughout this book, the lifeblood of lowriding—namely, cruising—would come to an end in the late 1970s. National City's Highland Avenue was the hub of cruising for San Diego lowriders. Law enforcement shut down Highland, they claimed, as a way to maintain law and order and support the local businesses; lowriders saw the shutdown as a form of harassment and discrimination against Chicano lowriders. After years of protest, debate and deliberations, National City passed an ordinance making it a crime to cruise. Cruising Control signs were posted on Highland Avenue. Hence, National City would go the way of countless cities with large lowrider populations that were systematically banning cruising in San Diego. Such an action would affect the meaning and expressions of lowriding forever because cruising was, and remains, at the heart and soul of lowriding.

The Code of Ordinances for National City, California, under Title 11: Vehicle and Traffic, Chapter 11.68.10, defines cruising as

> *the repetitive driving of a motor vehicle two or more times within a four-hour period, in the same direction, past a traffic control point in traffic which is congested at or near the traffic control point, as determined by the ranking police officer on duty within the affected area, and after the vehicle operator or passenger has been given an adequate written notice that further driving past the control point will be a violation of cruising.*

Top: Law enforcement officers make their presence known among lowriders at Mission Bay. *Courtesy of Richie Burgos.*

Bottom: Various members from different car clubs congregate in Otto Square after a protest cruise against the prohibition of cruising on Highland by law enforcement. *Courtesy of Ernie Carillo.*

Recently, National City officials have made attempts to mend the unfriendly environment that was produced between the city and the San Diego lowrider community with the shutting down of Highland Avenue.

City officials have sponsored and organized many community events that invite lowriders to come out and display their vehicles for a good cause. Most of these events are situated within parking lots of local grocery stores, and the general public is encouraged to attend. According to the Lowrider Community Advisory Council of National City, the objective of such events is to "bridge the gap between law enforcement, local car clubs, as well as community…[to] erase the negative stigma it has had throughout the years," according to advisory council member Mayra Nuñez. The San Diego lowrider community waits patiently to see what the future might hold for taking back the streets.

As a result, the shutting down of Highland Avenue shifted a good part of lowriding into the car show circuit. Building quality show cars for awards and praises introduced a new expression in the evolution of lowriding. In this chapter, we review a variety of car clubs that created stunning cars to adapt to the changing trends in lowriding and address some of the challenges and issues associated with this transformation.

Thee Crowd Car Club of National City

Steve "Masa" Wade, Rene Dumas and friends created Thee Crowd Car Club in 1980. The club has remained active over the years, organizing dances and fundraisers with as many as thirty-two members in the club at its peak. A significant contribution of Thee Crowd Car Club is the splash that its cars generated on the car show circuit. In the mid-1980s Masa introduced a new level of artistry in the lowrider community with his customized 1964 Buick Rivi "Beyond Imagination." It took the car show circuit by storm and placed customized lowriding into a field all its own. The complete modification of this impressive vehicle is referred to as "totally radicalized" in the custom car world. One of its signature qualities was its paint job by Benny Flores, described as "one of a kind."

"Beyond Imagination" won first place at numerous car shows and represents a good example of how lowriding abandoned the streets for the car show circuit. This magnificent car was sold to Gaspar Martinez in 1995 and transformed into "Timeless." It can be seen in lowrider car shows today. (The evolution and alterations of this vehicle are described in chapter 4 under the Casinos Car Club section. Its various stages of transformation are in the color insert pages.)

The founding members of Thee Crowd Car Club from National City, California. *Courtesy of Steve "Masa" Wade.*

The 1964 Buick Riviera "Beyond Imagination," owned by Steve "Masa" Wade of the Crowd Car Club. *Courtesy of Steve "Masa" Wade.*

Producing lowriders for cruising the streets versus the car show is an ongoing conversation that commenced during this era. As cruising sites became regulated and outlawed, the lowrider lifestyle was pushed into the car show.

Groupe Car Club of San Diego

By the mid-1970s, Allen "Butch" Sherman had joined City Car Club. In the early 1980s, he found himself traveling to East Los Angeles to meet with Groupe Car Club for permission to establish a San Diego chapter. He was granted permission as long as he could produce at least ten potential members who owned lowriders. Butch surpassed that request and gathered fifteen lowriders to create Groupe Car Club in 1981. Part of the club membership was composed of U.S. Marines who were stationed at Camp

A Groupe Car Club jacket wrapped around the front seat of Allen "Butch" Sherman's 1978 Ford Thunderbird. *Courtesy of Allen "Butch" Sherman.*

Pendleton in Oceanside. In addition to this military presence, there were members from throughout San Diego County, a distinctive element of the club. During this period, there were not many car clubs in North County, San Diego, so to have members from this area was unique. The lowriders in Groupe were characterized by their stock paint jobs, 520 tires, rims and lifted bodies. Butch owned an impressive 1978 Ford Thunderbird. The late 1980s brought changes to the car club, including members who served in the Marine Corps being transferred out of the area. Groupe is currently in its second or third generation and remains active with about ten members.

UNLIMITED CAR CLUB OF NATIONAL CITY

Ben Osorio was absorbed into lowrider culture. Not only was his brother an active lowrider, but Ben also lived on the corner of Highland Avenue and Twenty-Fourth Street, at the center of the cruising scene in San Diego. As a young man in junior high school, Ben distinguished himself by building

Members of Unlimited Car Club from National City, California, pose with their car club jackets. *Courtesy of Ben Osorio.*

A 1980 news article featuring customized bicycle show winner Benjamin Osorio, who later became a member of Unlimited Car Club. *Courtesy of Ben Osorio.*

lowrider bicycles and winning lowrider bike competitions. By 1983, while a student at Sweetwater High School in National City, Ben and his good friend George Yosif gathered some friends and established Unlimited Car Club. In addition to George and Ben, founding club members included Robert Martinez, Shaney Silvia, Rick Juan Casillas, Hector Gomez, Ismael Gomez and Eddie Solace. Club members already owned cars, which they would proudly drive to school to display for all to see. Friendship was key to this club, and lowriders were the reason why they hung out and cruised. A typical day of cruising would begin in Golden Hills and later in the day move to Chicano Park before ending at Sea Port Village in San Diego. The club produced many notable cars, including Ben Osorio's 1969 Chevy Impala. As the club members grew older, many married and were no longer available to continue with the club. The club still participates in car shows on a limited basis.

INDIVIDUALS CAR CLUB OF LOGAN HEIGHTS

During the early 1980s, Roberto "Beto" Sandoval and Ismael Arias were motivated to form a lowrider car club that represented lowriding through newer model vehicles. They looked for individuals who owned newer style lowrider cars and shared a similar vision. The unique characteristic of this emerging club was that with their extraordinarily customized lowrider vehicles, they would hit the streets just like any other car and be driven and cruised on a daily basis. Beto was attracted to the name of a lowrider car club out of Fresno, California, known as Thee Individuals, so the founding members, Beto and Ismael, in addition to Carlos Rojas, Juan Cuervo and Armando Medina, all gathered and decided to drop "Thee" and officially became Individuals Car Club. They continued to recruit members and had twenty-three by the mid-1980s. Individuals Car Club have produced some sophisticated and customized lowrider cars, including Alejandro Lemus's 1977 Monte Carlo "Purple Rain," Jesús Lemus's 1981 Monte Carlo "Red Monte For Show," Jesús Burgos's 1976 Monte Carlo "Axtec Alliance" and Ismael Arias's 1979 Pontiac Gran Prix.

A group picture of members of the Individuals Car Club. *Courtesy of Armando Medina.*

Individuals Car Club members participate in a 1989 San Bernardino Car Show. *Courtesy of Armando Medina.*

Individuals Car Club continues to meet at Chicano Park in Logan Heights. The club has been meeting at the park since 1982. The club is motivated by a strong sense of family that expresses respect and love for one another. Individuals Car Club remains active in the San Diego lowrider car scene with a total of nineteen active members.

Rag Tops Car Club of San Diego

Raul Rodriguez grew up in a lowrider family and spent his early years in Logan Heights. Around 1982, he organized guys from Logan Heights and Sherman Heights to create a distinct car club composed of convertibles known as the Rag Tops Car Club. "Convertibles are unique," said Raul. "The wind in your hair, loud music, everyone can see you, and you can see everyone." As he imagined the feeling of cruising a lowrider, he thought, what better way to experience a cruise than in a rag top? Part of the challenge was to locate convertible cars and customize them into lowriders. Raul's tenacity paid off, and he was able to pull together a group of lowrider

"Moving Violation," a 1964 Impala convertible that belonged to Norman Paraiso of the Rag Tops Lowrider Car Club. *Courtesy of Raul Rodriguez.*

This 1959 Chevy Impala convertible belonged to Raul Rodriguez from the Rag Tops Lowrider Car Club. *Courtesy of Raul Rodriguez.*

Bishop Leo T. Maher and Sebastiano Cardinal Baggio of the Vatican ride in the backseat of a customized convertible owned by the Rag Tops during a religious celebration of the Virgin of Guadalupe at Our Lady of Guadalupe Church in Logan Heights. *Courtesy of Raul Rodriguez.*

convertibles with enthusiastic owners who were ready to hit the streets. Founding members included Raul Rodriguez, Alfredo Zavala, Smokey Ayala, Carlos Uribe, Joaquin Flores Sr. and Jose Garibay. One of the most notable cars from this club is Raul's 1959 Chevy Impala convertible. It was a very popular vehicle in the car show circuit, winning numerous trophies and distinctions.

As noted earlier in this chapter, this era marks the end of the lowrider car scene that we identify as foundational. There are many changes occurring in both the lowrider street scene and within the Chicano barrio. The U.S. economy was in a deep recession with high unemployment, close to 11 percent. The Chicano community was especially hit hard, with conflicts flaring up between communities and rival street gangs. It was within this context that Rag Tops Car Club entered the lowrider scene, conscious of the harsh realities on the streets of Chicano barrios in San Diego and wishing to offer hope through an imaginative way to cruise the streets.

The car club became extremely popular in accompanying *quinceañeras* and escorting the parties via a car caravan to the church and celebration. As discussed in an earlier chapter, lowriding and religion have been interconnected in lowrider history. Rag Tops was very popular with Father Brown from Our Lady of Guadalupe Church in Logan Heights. The year

Street Vistas
CRUISIN' WITH MASA

It was late Friday night as Steve "Masa" Wade was putting the finishing touches on some bodywork on his 1965 Chevy Impala, getting ready to take it out for a cruise on Highland Avenue. To his dismay, he had run out of Bondo and found himself pressured to finish the job he had started in order to get together with his friends who were waiting for him impatiently at his house. He ran into the house and noticed his mother had prepared *masa*, or dough, for tortillas or tamales. Without skipping a beat, Steve took a good portion of his mother's masa, combined it with a hardener and, like magic, successfully resolved his problem. After applying it to his vehicle, he proceeded to quickly sand it and then applied primer paint, and before you knew it, he was cruising Highland with his friends. As he was swept up by the excitement of the evening cruise, he hit the switches and began to hop his ride, and soon after, the motion of the car caused his creative concoction to crash onto the street pavement. As friends and fellow cruisers rushed over to inspect the strange mixture scattered throughout, it is alleged that one person yelled out, "Hey, that looks like masa!" From that point forward, Steve Wade was called Masa.

1992 marks the transitional period in Rag Tops with the untimely passing of Ramón Loretto Legge. Club members deeply mourned his passing, and they remained dormant until 2013, when the second generation stepped up to move the club into its next chapter.

Like everything in life, the end of an era evokes nostalgia and sadness in the hearts of those who lived it. It is not our intent to induce such sentiments in the writing of this book. Instead, we wish to respectfully suggest that you must write your own history for it to endure, as we have done in writing this book. Therefore, we advocate that all lowrider movements, their clubs and participants, write their history so that all their challenges and hard work will not be in vain and the stories of joy and struggle will continue to keep the movement alive for years to come.

Conclusion

THE FUTURE OF LOWRIDING

Taking to the Streets in a Global World

M any things occurred in the 1980s that changed and transformed
cruising forever. First and foremost, Highland Avenue was
systematically shut down by law enforcement, and similar actions took
place throughout the borderlands with active lowrider communities. As
stated previously, open and public spaces to cruise and gather would quickly
disappear. Secondly, *Lowrider* magazine was sold by its founder, Sonny

Richie Burgos of Latin Lowriders Car Club. *Courtesy of Marvin Israel Berechyahu Mayorga.*

San Diego Lowrider Council Annual Picnic 2016. *Courtesy of Marvin Israel Berechyahu Mayorga.*

Madrid, and the magazine that created a way for lowriders to connect and be informed about the movement in general was gone. Finally, a new car movement came on the San Diego car scene: the mini-truck. Around 1983, the mini-truck movement took hold because of the vehicle's affordability, and members of this new car movement began to adapt specific lowrider style and technology to their vehicles. For example, customized hydraulic beds that would move and groove became attractive for many. These fancy trucks would be customized with impressive paint jobs, interiors and suicide doors. The lower-profile tires and rims were also adapted into this new movement. Eventually, new car clubs within the lowrider movement would be born, such as Sweet N Low and Friends Mini Trucks car clubs. The mini-trucks movement was supported by a new and younger generation of car enthusiasts and car customizers. In addition, these new clubs were more ethnically diverse than the traditional lowrider car clubs. The modified mini-truck expression would go strong until the mid-1990s. All three of these occurrences detoured the foundational lowrider movement.

In reflecting back to the early days of young Mexican Americans and Chicanos taking to the streets and customizing vehicles to make a statement about themselves, one would have never imagined that this distinctive expression that came out of American Southwest barrios would now be an international phenomenon. Today, the lowrider movement in all its forms can be found in Germany, Brazil and Japan, just to name a few. The Japanese lowrider movement is important because it has been around for the past thirty years, and several of these car clubs have reached out and contacted San Diego lowriders. The Pharaohs lowrider car club from Nagoya, Japan,

Esmeralda Car Club of northern Japan, 2015. *Courtesy of Rigo Reyes.*

is one of the oldest Japanese lowrider car clubs. It has spent time on the San Diego lowrider car scene, exchanging ideas and learning more about the art and history of lowriding. The Esmeralda Car Club of northern Japan has also spent time in San Diego, making contacts with the lowrider car scene and bringing the art of low and slow between Japan and Southern California closer together. In Japan, different lowrider styles are influenced by regions.

In March 2015, thirty delegates representing San Diego lowrider culture traveled to Port Messe, Nagoya, Japan, to participate in the Classic Legends Lowrider and Kustom Car Show at the invitation of the Japanese lowrider community and promoter Oryu Oreo. This event was the largest indoor car show in the world, with lowriders representing every corner of the world. Most importantly is that this unprecedented event and gathering took place in Japan. Several of the participants noted from their experience that the Japanese lowrider community showed nothing but love and respect for Chicano culture, admiration for Chicano Park and the lowrider lifestyle. The San Diego lowrider delegation witnessed "high quality workmanship and development" from the Japanese lowrider community that they refer to as "oversees-builders." As one of the San Diego delegates, Bobby Ruiz, said, "Both the technical skills and quality of the Japanese lowrider has improved over the years and is now on par with lowriders imagined and built in the United States."

The future of lowriding is filled with new roads and new vistas. The legacy and contributions of the lowrider movement and its people are too strong and robust to be contained within the barrios of *Aztlán* and the borderlands. The sky is the limit for the new creations and variations that will spring forth from the minds of women and men who make up the lowrider world. Yet we caution all who partake in or admire this exceptional movement that they take the time to learn the history and substance of the lowrider movement as we have attempted to present in this book. Our hope is that this book has offered a historical and intellectual roadmap and provided a historical grounding that we hope will inform and guide both the participant and enthusiast in learning the special qualities of lowriding. In the end, the art of low and slow is more than a fad; it is a way of life. See you on the streets.

GLOSSARY

The purpose of this glossary is to define key concepts presented in the book that may not be familiar to all readers. It is presented in a narrative format in an attempt to integrate these key terms into the cultural expressions that come out of the lowrider movement.

We begin with the concept of *Chicano* or *Chicana*, which describes Mexican-origin people from the late 1960s through the 1980s who were activists for civil rights and social justice. *Chicanismo* is the philosophy to commit oneself to live and uphold the values and vision of the Chicano movement. *Mexican Americans* are individuals who recognize their Mexican and American ancestry. Finally, *Mexicans* are individuals born in Mexico and live in the United States or in Mexico. They have great pride in their Mexican roots and origins. All three terms are used interchangeably in the barrios and communities of the American Southwest and borderlands and speak to the *raíces*, or "roots," of this ethnic community.

Several cultural values are introduced in the introduction such as *persona educada*, interpreted as "educated people" but in a more holistic sense. *Sentimientos de orgullo* are sentiments of pride. *Respeto* is respect. *Consejos* are advice, and *amor propio* is self-love. All represent traditional Mexican values.

A *barrio* is a historic neighborhood composed mainly of people of Mexican origin throughout the United States. El Paso, Santa Barbara, Los Angeles and San Diego have historic barrios that go back many years. Two of San Diego's historic barrios are San Ysidro and Logan Heights. A *colonia* is a neighborhood found within Mexican cities like Tijuana. One of the most famous *colonias* in Tijuana is *La Colonia Libertad*.

A *pocho* is an anglicized Mexican, a derogatory term used by Mexicans to differentiate themselves from less acculturated Mexicans. It is commonly heard in the borderlands region or in Mexico. A *veterano* is an elder, or literally a "veteran" of the lowrider movement. They are said to possess a great deal of knowledge and wisdom and are to be treated with respect.

A *ranfla* is Caló for car or, more specifically, a customized lowrider. The term is commonly used by members of the lowrider community.

The concept of *frontera* refers to the U.S.-Mexico border from the perspective of the Mexican. It literally translates to frontier. The relationship and interaction of people from both sides of the border (San Diego–Tijuana) are emphasized in this book, and thus, the term borderlands provides a more accurate depiction of the region throughout history. *Aztlán* is the ancient homeland of the Mexica or Aztec people that became popular during the Chicano civil rights movement to refer to the territories of the American Southwest that historically were part of Mexico.

Lowriders organize themselves as car clubs, and we utilize the label of *clica*, or "clique," to acknowledge such clubs. *Compadrazgo* represents a form of sponsorship that was popular between lowrider clubs from San Diego and Tijuana. A *compadre* or *comadre* is literally a godfather or godmother who offers support beyond the immediate family in times of need.

Bibliography

Amato, Joseph. "Local History: A Way to Place and Home." In *Why Place Matters*, edited by Wilfred M. McClay and Ted V. McAllister, 215–37. New York: New Atlantis Books, 2014.

Camarillo, Mateo. *An Immigrant's Journey in Search of the American Dream*. San Diego, CA: self-published, 2014.

Chappell, Ben. *Aesthetics and Politics of Mexican American Custom Cars: Lowrider Space*. Austin: University of Texas Press, 2012.

Everything Comes from the Streets. Directed by Alberto López Pulido. DVD. San Diego, CA: San Diego Audio Video, 2014.

García, Maria E. "The History of Neighborhood House in Logan Heights: 1950s Social Clubs—Los Gallos." *San Diego Free Press*, May 23, 2015. http://sandiegofreepress.org/2015/05/the-history-of-neighborhood-house-in-logan-heights-1950s-social-clubs-los-gallos.

"Iconic *Lowrider* Magazine Unveils New Identity Through Redesigned Magazine and Website." TEN, October 15, 2015. http://www.enthusiastnetwork.com/iconic-lowrider-magazine-unveils-new-identity-redesigned-magazine-website.

Madrigal, Juan Antonio Del Monte. *Entre Ruedas y Asfalto: Identidades y Movilidades de Bikers y Lowriders en Tijuana*. Tijuana, MX: El Colef, 2014.

National City, California. Code of Ordinances. https://www.municode.com/library/ca/national_city/codes/code_of_ordinances?nodeId=CD_ORD_TIT11VETR.

Penland, Paige R. *Lowrider: History, Pride, Culture*. St. Paul, MN: Motorbooks, 2003.

"The Perfect Stance." *Custom Car Chronicles: The Beauty of Customizing*, February 18, 2016. http://www.customcarchronicle.com/custom-history/the-perfect-stance.

Pluss, Marilyn Teyssier. "Before Imperial Beach, The City." http://coib. govoffice2.com/vertical/Sites/%7B6283CA4C-E2BD-4DFA-A7F7-8D4ECD543E0F%7D/uploads/%7BF77D2AE6-AD4B-45DA-954F-4E9D8837B82C%7D.PDF.

Pulido, Alberto López. "San Diego Lowriders Go Global." *La Prensa*, February 27, 2015. http://laprensa-sandiego.org/featured/san-diego-lowriders-go-global.

Reyes, Rigoberto. "Amigos Car Club: Chicano Park in Japan." Forty-fifth-annual Chicano Park Program, 2015.

San Diego Union Tribune. "Drag-Racing Pioneer Cofounded Bean Bandits Club." October 8, 2010.

Sandoval, Denise. "Bajito y Suavecito: The Lowriding Tradition." Smithsonian Institution, 2003. http://latino.si.edu/virtualgallery/lowrider/lr_sandovalessay.htm.

Tatum, Charles M. *Lowriders in Chicano Culture: From Low to Slow to Show*. Santa Barbara, CA: Greenwood, 2011.

Zaragoza, Barbara. "Lowriders Return to Highland Avenue in National City." *San Diego Free Press*, August 5, 2015. http://sandiegofreepress. org/2015/08/lowriders-return-to-highland-avenue-in-national-city.

INDEX

About the Authors

ALBERTO LÓPEZ PULIDO grew up along the *frontera* of San Diego–Tijuana, where he learned a great deal about culture and tradition in a bicultural, bilingual and binational world. His greatest influences in life have been his mother and grandfather, who taught him the deep values of holistic education that go beyond formal education. Alberto is a proud graduate of the University of Notre Dame's Mexican American Graduate Studies Program, which was established by Professor Julian Samora. Alberto is a professor of ethnic studies at the University of San Diego and served as its founding chair. He has numerous publications in the subjects of Chicano Religions, higher education and border studies. Alberto is an award-winning documentary filmmaker with his directorial debut of *Everything Comes from the Streets: A History of Lowriding in San Diego California and the Borderlands*. It was awarded first place at the Barrio Film Festival and a distinguished Remi Award at WorldFest: Houston International Film Festival. The documentary also premiered at Cine+Mas Film Festival in San Francisco; CineFestival, San Antonio; Watsonville Film Festival; and Ethnografilm International Film Festival, Paris, France. It secured two television broadcasts: KPBS, San

Courtesy of Nick Abadilla.

Diego, and KQED "Truly California" Series, San Francisco. *Everything Comes from the Streets* was coproduced with Pulido's coauthor, Rigoberto Reyes, and award-winning filmmaker Kelly Whalen.

RIGOBERTO (RIGO) REYES was born in San Diego in 1957. For the past thirty years, he has worked for Via International, where he coordinates and implements community development projects and is responsible for developing and training leadership skills to people in marginal areas of the cities of Tijuana and San Diego. Rigo oversees and assists in developing human potential with *promotoras*, or "outreach workers," who volunteer their time to improve their communities. As a young boy during the civil rights movement, Rigo grew up in San Ysidro in the midst of the rallies of the United Farm Workers of America listening to César Chávez. At the

Courtesy of Diana Wolf.

age of twelve, Rigo drove his bike seventeen miles each way from his barrio to the Logan Heights community to witness the takeover of a little piece of land by the community that today is known as Chicano Park. It was from this experience that his love for activism and social justice was born. Rigo has been an active lowrider since 1975. He began as a member of the Casinos Car Club and then became a founding member and former president of Amigos Car Club. He is also cofounder of the San Diego Lowrider Council, established in 1979. Rigo was copublisher and editor of *Vivo Magazine "La Voz del Barrio"* from 1981 to 1983, and he assisted in the establishment of the Balboa Park Automotive Museum. In 2002, he coproduced for San Diego County TV the documentary *Amigos Car Club* and, in 2013, coproduced the award-winning documentary *Everything Comes from the Streets*. Rigo is a former board member of the Centro Cultural de la Raza in Balboa Park and currently serves as a board member of the Chicano Park Museum and Cultural Center. He is a longtime member of the Chicano Park Steering Committee in San Diego, *Califas*. Rigo is currently a professor of practice at the University of San Diego, where he is teaching a course on immigration.

CPSIA information can be obtained
at www.ICGtesting.com
Printed in the USA
LVOW02*1155080517

533706LV00010B/644/P